Faces of the USA

Elizabeth Laird

Photography by Darryl Williams

Longman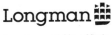

London and New York

The United States of America

There are fifty states in the United States of America. Some, like Texas and Alaska, are very big. Others, like Delaware and Maryland, are small. The United States covers a huge area of the North American continent. It is about 1,600 miles from north to south, and about 3,000 miles from east to west.

Two states are geographically separate from the others. These are Alaska, a huge, snowy region to the northwest of Canada, and Hawaii, a group of beautiful tropical islands in the Pacific Ocean. (Alaska and Hawaii are not shown on the map.)

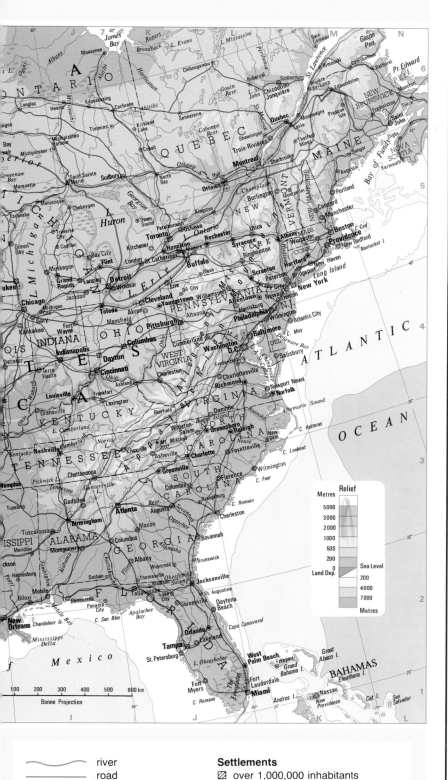

Contents

Longman Group UK Limited,
Longman House, Burnt Mill, Harlow,
Essex CM20 2JE, England
and Associated Companies throughout the world.

Published in the United States of America
by Longman Inc., New York

First published 1987
Fourth impression 1991

British Library Cataloging-in-Publication Data
Laird, Elizabeth
Faces of the U.S.A.
1. United States—Social life and customs—1971–
I. Title   II. Williams, Darryl
973′.927   E169.04

ISBN 0-582-74923-9

Library of Congress Cataloging-in-Publication Data
Laird, Elizabeth, 1943—Faces of the U.S.A.
1. Readers—United States.
2. English language—Text-books for foreign speakers.
3. United States—Social life and customs.
I. Title.   II. Title: Faces of the USA.
PE1127.H5L27   1987   428.6′4   87–4069

Set in 9/12pt Cheltenham Light

Produced by Longman Group (FE) Ltd.
Printed in Hong Kong

Acknowledgements

We are grateful to the following for permission to
reproduce copyright photographs:

Adams Picture Library for page 72; All-Sport (UK)
Limited for pages 66 (bottom left and right) and 67; Art
Directors Photo Library for page 10; Coca-Cola Limited
for page 62; Colorific Photo Library Limited for pages 5,
Alan Reininger/Contact Press Images/Colorific for page
15 (left), Harry Seawell/Black Star/Colorific for page 49,
Tom Craig/Black Star/Colorific for page 60, Darrell-
Jones/Contact Press Images/Colorific for page 65,
Richard Howard/Black Star/Colorific for page 68; Darrell-
Jones Contact Press Images/Colorific for the cover
(bottom right), Robert Harding Picture Library Limited
for pages 51 (left) and 54 (bottom); The Image Bank
for pages 23 (middle), 46, 50, 58, and 74; The
Photographers Library for page 33; The Photo Source for
page 30 (top); Pictor International Limited for page 30
(bottom); Rex Features Limited for page 56 (top); Tony
Stone Photo Library/London for page 78.
The map on pages 2 and 3 © Collins-Longman Atlases.
All other photographs by Darryl Williams.
Illustration by Per Dahlberg.

Chapter One

The American People

Faces in the crowd

Black, white, rich, poor, Jew, Christian, Muslim, Irish, Italian, Chinese, Hispanic, Russian, German, Japanese, African—you will find them all in the U.S.A. The great American idea has always been that all these people should become something new. They should leave their old lives behind and become American.

In some ways, the idea has worked. Many people have forgotten where their grandparents came from. They share the ideas, experiences, and feelings that make up the American culture. But new questions are now being asked. Some people wonder if too much has been lost. They are becoming more interested in the countries their families once left. They are not sure if new immigrants should try to forget their own languages and cultures so completely.

Americans talk a great deal about how wonderful it is to be American. The reason may be because they need to keep reminding themselves that that is what they are.

The First Americans

With beauty all around me

You probably know the romantic names of the most famous American Indian tribes: Apache, Sioux, Cherokee, and Comanche. They probably make you think of men riding horses with feathers in their hair, and women with long, plaited hair and soft leather dresses. But there are, in fact, hundreds of tribes of Indians, all with different customs. Some have always lived in houses and grown their own food. Some used to move from place to place and hunt animals. Some were fishermen, living by the sea.

But although the Indian tribes are very different, they all share the same love and respect for nature. They believe that each living thing is as precious as every other living thing.

"Nothing is simple and alone," said a priest of the Pueblo Indians. "The breathing mountains, the living stones, each blade of grass, the clouds, the rain, each star, the beasts, the birds, and the spirits of the air—we are all one."

When the Europeans came, the Indians watched with horror as the forests were cut down, the prairie grasses ploughed up, and the wild animals destroyed. They themselves were slowly driven off the good land. Sometimes they fought, but white people had better weapons and always won in the end. Sometimes they made agreements, but the white man always broke his promises. Some

tribes died out completely, and were lost forever. The darkest hour of the American Indians was at Wounded Knee, South Dakota, in 1890, when 200 Sioux were shot. The American Indians had finally been beaten.

Since then, the Indian story has been tragic. Indians have been given only poor pieces of land, called "reservations," on which to live. Even that land has often been taken away, as coal and oil have been discovered beneath it. Many Indians experience a terrible sadness for what they have lost. Forty percent are unemployed, and most are poor. Twice as many young Indians as white people take their own lives. Many have serious alcohol problems.

But at the same time, white people have been learning a few things. Some feel ashamed of what their people have done to the Indians. Some, especially young people, regret the poisoned rivers, the lost forests, and the disappearing wild animals. They have started to respect Indian beliefs and customs, such as the dances through which they reach the spirits. They have begun to enjoy Indian poetry, like this Navajo prayer for healing:

With beauty before me, I walk
With beauty behind me, I walk
With beauty below me, I walk
With beauty above me, I walk
With beauty all around me, I walk.

Florence Aguino from San Juan Pueblo

Florence Aguino speaks two languages: Tewa, the language of her Indian people, and English, which she learned at school. She also understands Spanish. She lives with her family on the San Juan reservation in New Mexico, the home of about 1,300 Pueblo Indians. She works part-time as a hairdresser, and she also teaches art and crafts to senior citizens in the "pueblo," the Indian village community in which she lives.

It isn't easy to get Florence to talk about herself. She's more used to thinking about other people, especially her family.

Indian village at Mesa Verde, Colorado

"Our families are the most important thing about our life in the pueblo," she says. "My family is still close to each other, but some families are breaking up. The closeness has gone. That's sad."

Florence believes that without a strong family, the Indian way of life will disappear. She herself learned so much from her parents. The Aguinos were a well-known dancing family, and her father sang the old Indian songs to the children from the day they were born. As soon as they could walk, they started to learn the religious dances.

"My dad taught Ben, my son, too," says Florence. "He has danced the deer dance since he was one year old. And he can do the buffalo, the butterfly, the cloud, the turtle, the peace pipe, and the Comanche. We dance on special days, on feast days. The dancing is very important to me. We dance to have good crops, to have a good year, for different things."

Florence remembers, too, that her father told wonderful stories when she was little. They had no electricity in those days. Ten of them lived in the small two-roomed house. They used to sit around the fire, and listen to the stories of the corn maiden and the red fox, and of the old days, hundreds of years ago, when the Spanish first came.

"Now we have television, we don't tell the stories anymore," says Florence, "and not so many people speak the Tewa language."

Florence's father was a leader in the San Juan pueblo, but when he died, Florence became the head of her family. She is responsible for her brother, in the hospital with a serious drinking problem. She also looks after her elderly mother. She would never let her go to a nursing home.

"We Indians respect our old people," she says. "That's what I teach my children, the same that my mom and dad taught me, to respect others and make them respect you too."

Above left:
Traditional 3-dimensional painting by Florence's brother Juan, with (inset) a photograph of her son
Above right:
Florence Aguino at her home in San Juan pueblo

Young People

Teenage girls

"A Country of Young Men?"

What's your idea of a typical American child? Rather noisy, perhaps? With too many expensive toys, a mouth full of chewing gum, and no respect for adults? A child who's never happy except when watching television? Yes, maybe. But most American children are also full of energy and confidence, ready to go out and make their own way in the world.

What's your idea of a typical American teenager? A rich kid with his own car? A girl whose parents let her do anything she likes? A drug addict? Well, maybe you have been watching too much television yourself. Most teenagers do not have enough money to own their own car. Drugs, of course, are a serious problem, but the truth is that fewer and fewer young Americans are trying them. In 1978, as many as 10 percent of high-school seniors smoked marijuana every day. Now fewer than 5 percent have the habit. New drug-users are often older people, in their twenties and thirties.

Typical American teenagers are in fact very ordinary. They think their teachers make them work too hard, they love their parents but are sure they don't understand anything, and their friendships are the most important things in their lives. Some of them do have a lot of money to spend, but usually they have earned it themselves. Most young people take jobs while they are in school. They work at movie theaters, fast-food restaurants, gas stations, and stores to pay for their clothes and entertainment. Maybe this is what makes them so independent from their parents at such a young age.

It isn't always easy to keep a job, and still do well in school. But American children learn early that you have to work hard to win. Winning, in fact, is part of the American way of life. Americans just love competitions, even in their time off. Few people can enjoy a sport unless they are trying to beat someone else at it.

"America," wrote Emerson, the nineteenth-century writer, "is a country of young men." That's not quite true anymore. The population is growing older. Fewer and fewer babies are being born, and baby food factories are closing down. America does not belong to young people anymore, in the way it did only twenty years ago. Young people today are having to fight harder to get the kinds of jobs and homes they want. Maybe that is why young Americans are more serious now than they used to be. They have less time for fun and sun these days. Now it's all work, work, work.

David Goode

David Goode—
A Simple Ambition

David Goode, seventeen years old, is the kind of young man most parents would like their daughter to go out with. But they would be too late. He has a girlfriend already. He and Julie met fifteen months ago, at their local Catholic church, and they've been dating ever since. David is quite romantic about it.

"It seems like we haven't been dating that long, because every moment has been wonderful," he says.

It's not surprising that David met Julie at church, because religion is important to him. He goes to mass every Sunday. But he doesn't leave his faith behind when he goes out through the church doors.

"I think I'm like my parents," says David. "They're very active in the church. My father's a pacifist, and I agree with him. I don't believe in war at all. I don't want to do anything like joining the army. The important thing in a job is having fun, but also helping others, having a real purpose, seeing results."

David has had plenty of jobs already. He's enjoyed most of them. His sense of humor has made sure of that. He started at fourteen, and since then he's worked in a Jewish delicatessen, a fast-food place, and a restaurant. Now he's working in a movie theater, taking tickets and sweeping and cleaning the lobby. One day, though, when David has finished college, he wants to go into business. He doesn't want to be rich, exactly, but he'd like to be well-off. He's had a good start. He spends only part of the money he earns on dances, gifts, and sodas. The rest he is carefully saving, and his dad is helping to invest it wisely. It will help to pay for his college education.

David knows what he wants and how he's going to get it. It's not surprising that his favorite sport is long-distance running.

"It would be so easy to stop running," he says. "When I'm doing it, I repeat a song to myself, or a math equation, just to keep myself going."

But David isn't going to stop. He has seen what family problems and drugs have done to some of his friends. But he's going to be more careful. He's going to do what his parents did—settle down early, make a good marriage, find a good job, do it well, and have a large family. He's going to pass on to his children the wish to help others that he has learned from his parents. He's going to be the backbone of America.

Working Women

"Here they are, home from school," said the soft voice on TV. "Uh-oh, look at those shirts. How is mom ever going to get them white again?"

The message was clear. Buy our soap powder, Mrs. America, and you will be a good mother. The next advertisements were not very different. "Buy our frozen food," they said, "or our floor polish, or our perfume. You will be a good cook, a good homemaker, and your husband will always love you."

Thirty years ago, Americans had a clear picture of how they thought women should be. The perfect woman was the happy, bright homemaker in one of the new, middle-class suburbs. She had a washing machine and a vacuum cleaner to make her work easy. She had plenty of time to make her home beautiful, cook delicious meals for her husband and children, and be everyone's friend and adviser.

This advertiser's dream of American women still exists on TV, but it is far from the real truth. For one thing, one in ten women chooses not to marry at all. And fewer and fewer families now look like the advertisers' picture of a mother, a father, and two children. By 1980, one in every five families in the U.S.

A family home in a middle-class suburb

had only one parent, and the number of "single-parent families" continues to rise. Women on their own with children cannot afford to stay at home. They have to find work in order to feed their families.

At the same time, the married woman in her beautiful suburban house has begun to feel bored. She is tired of staying at home all day to cook, clean, and sew. Many women have decided to go out and find a job. In 1950, two out of every three women stayed home. By 1985, two out of three women over the age of sixteen were working outside the home.

Finding jobs may help women in some ways, but life is still not perfect. Women still earn much less than men. For every dollar a man can earn, a woman only earns sixty cents. And going out to work has not made housework any easier. Women must still cook and clean after a hard day in the office or the factory. Although some American husbands are happy to help, most working women do more than twice as much housework as men.

None of this worries Junior, when he meets his mom coming home from work. "Just look at your shirt!" she says. "How ever am I going to get it white again?"

Nancy Wesley—Hopes for a Better Future

What do you do when you are a woman with two young children? You spend a lot of time and energy looking after them. What do you do when you're also divorced and have no money? You have to look after the children and earn enough money to feed and clothe them. What happens if you are also only twenty-four years old, and have hopes and dreams for a better life in the future? You look after the children, go out to work, and go to college, all at the same time. That has been Nancy Wesley's way of life for two years now.

Nancy gets up at 6:00 every morning, dresses four-year-old Matthew, and two-year-old Anna, and fixes their breakfast. At 8:00 she takes them to the baby-sitter, who has two

children of her own. Then she goes to school, and takes classes from 8:30 until 2:30. At 3:00 she picks up the children, and spends time with them at home. Two hours later, at 5:00, it's time to go to the Wal-mart store where she works in the sports department, selling hunting equipment such as guns and fishing rods. She's home around 10:00, and then she tries to study. On weekends Nancy's ex-husband takes the children, and she works all day on Saturday and Sunday in the store. She's always tired.

There's one thing that keeps Nancy going. She's determined to get her graduate degree, however difficult it is.

"The best thing in my life is the goal of my future, and working for that," she says. The other important thing is the children.

"They're super, super intelligent," Nancy says proudly. "It's been real tough for them. I feel bad about it. I know I get impatient with

them sometimes. Sure, I have regrets about it. I don't want them to do what I did. I want them to graduate and get a good home before they have kids."

Nancy is going to graduate next year, and then, she hopes, she'll get a better job, and have more time for the children. Maybe she'll be able to do some of the things that she did before, like playing tennis, or ice skating. She used to love sports, but she just doesn't have the energy anymore.

And who knows? Someday she might even get married again. Her first marriage lasted only two years, and when it ended she was left to pick up the pieces. Next time, she'll know better.

"Women have got to know how to look after themselves," she says. "We've got to learn to be more independent."

Nancy has learned the hard way.

Nancy Wesley at work in the sports department of a Wal-mart store

Old People

Seventy Years Young

"I'm seventy years old," says the gray-haired lady proudly to the entertainer at her Community Club dinner.

"Did you hear that, everyone?" says the entertainer. "This lovely lady is just seventy years *young*! And she doesn't look a day over fifty."

He has been careful not to use the word "old." In a society where youth is so admired, old age is often seen as something sad, something to fight against. Americans prefer not to say "old people." They use the expression "senior citizens." They do not talk about "old people's" homes, but "retirement" homes.

In fact, the entertainer is not so wrong. Seventy is not very old these days. People in the U.S. are living longer and longer. In 1980, 12 percent of Americans were over sixty-five years old. By 2030, 21 percent will be over sixty-five. One reason for this is that families are getting smaller. The average couple now has only 1.8 children. At the same time, improved medical care means that people are living longer.

This change in the age of Americans is going to have serious results. For one thing, medical costs are rising. The government's Medicare program aims to pay the medical costs of elderly people who cannot afford private insurance. But the bills have gone up so much that the money is running out. Some unfortunate old people have to leave hospital "sicker and quicker" than they should, before they are really better.

More fortunate senior citizens, though, who still have good health, are becoming more demanding at work. In the past, the retirement age was sixty-five, but that is changing now. Older people are stronger and more energetic than ever before. Many of them refuse to stop working just because they have reached a certain age. They want new laws to be passed to allow them to stay at work.

There is a change, too, in the way in which elderly people see themselves. Many are no longer happy to accept the gray hair, bald heads, and boring clothes of their own parents. They like to wear younger-looking fashions and bright makeup. American women spend millions of dollars a year on operations to lift their faces and make those ugly wrinkles disappear. Men are prepared to spend even more on operations to plant new hair on their bald spots. It's worth any money to look younger.

Sara Smith—Senior Citizen

If you try to phone Sara Smith, you'll be lucky to catch her at home. Take this week for example. On Monday, she played cards with a group of friends. On Tuesday, she went to a meeting of her book club. On Wednesday night, there was a big concert downtown. On Thursday, she went to spend the night with a younger friend, and on Friday, she went to the 150th birthday party of a local church. On Sunday, of course, she went to church, as she has done all her life.

Sara is seventy-seven, and since her husband died, she has lived alone. But that doesn't stop her doing more than most forty year olds. She drives herself around in a big, ten-year-old car, and she does everything for herself.

"I keep house, I do all my cooking," she says, looking around her beautiful home where you would have to look hard to find any dust. "I make all the clothes I wear, I read a lot, I talk on the telephone a lot, I watch television a lot—there's never a dull moment."

Sara wouldn't like to be young today. "My grandchildren have a difficult time," she says. "They're great kids, but there's such a difference between their home and the world in which they live. It was so different when I was young."

It certainly was. Sara remembers the first car that came to town. She also remembers the first plane she ever saw. It crashed in a cotton field near their home, and her father left his office to get his wife and children so they could come and see it.

The state of Georgia, where Sara lives, has probably changed more than most. Sara can remember visiting her grandparents on their old cotton plantation, near Augusta, Georgia. Two black servants served their breakfast, two others served their lunch, and two more served them at dinner. The servants' houses behind the big plantation house were still called the "slave quarters."

"Georgia has changed a lot, and for the better. It's grown so rapidly. It's a beautiful state, with beautiful highways and marvelous large cities. I was raised in a little country

Sara Smith at her home in Avondale, Georgia

town, with about a thousand people. We went to Savannah for special shopping. But in our little town, almost everybody was related."

Sara smiles at her memories, and shakes her head.

"No," she says. "I wouldn't like to be young today."

Rich and Poor

The Best for Some

All over the world, Americans are known for their easy way of spending money. Abroad, they often stay in the best hotels and go to the most expensive stores. At home, too, they are used to the best of everything. An ordinary American house has two bathrooms, a separate bedroom for each child, a garage, and several TV sets. Most families have a car, and many have a mobile home. Kitchens are full of expensive electrical appliances.

Americans work hard for their wealth, and they enjoy it. They respect people who have become millionaires. They enjoy watching TV programs and reading about the super-rich, the "big spenders." They admire women who can buy dresses for over $20,000, and rich businesspeople who can travel in their own private airplanes or even railroad cars.

People like to feel that they, too, could be rich if they worked hard enough. They feel good about the future. Most Americans say they are better off now than they were five years ago. To be free to do well, to be rewarded properly for honest, hard work— this, they say, is the real meaning of America. It was to this country, after all, that the poor of the world came to find a new life and a fair chance for their children, and many of them found it.

But not all. In recent years, more and more people have become trapped in an "under-class." Many, but not all of them, are black. Many, but not all, live in the old "inner" cities. These people seem to be unable to escape from bad housing, unemployment, and a life of crime and hopelessness. For them, drugs and alcohol are especially serious problems.

The numbers are surprising. By 1980, 12 percent of all American children belonged to families whose only income came from welfare programs. In some inner-city areas, over half the young people are unemployed. A recent government study has shown that one in eight Americans cannot read or write.

Politicians cannot decide on how to improve the situation. Some ask for more welfare payments for the poor, for better housing, more free food, better medical help. Others feel that the poor will only learn to help themselves if they receive no help at all from others.

Americans have always loved stories about poor people who worked hard and reached the top. They find it much harder to accept the idea of poor people who have no hope, no work to do, and who have to stay at the bottom.

The Baglady . . .

It's 8 o'clock on a Sunday morning in the Bowery district of New York City. Anna comes out of the shelter for the homeless where she has spent the night. She carries everything she owns in three plastic bags. She walks a little unsteadily down the street to a Chinese coffee shop. The owner, Mr. Chang, is good to the people who live on the streets. He often has a cup of tea and a pastry ready for them on Sunday morning. He doesn't ask to be paid.

Anna can't remember much about the past. She spent most of her early life in a mental hospital. "I've always been kind of nervous," she says. A few years ago a doctor decided she didn't need to stay in the hospital anymore.

"You're free to go," he told her. The trouble was, Anna didn't have anywhere to go. She moved from one cheap hotel to the next. She forgot to take the medicines the doctor had given her. She forgot to ask for more when she lost them.

Outside the coffee shop, there's a long line of hungry men and women. One of them is already drunk. He's making a speech. The gray, dirty people listen with enjoyment.

"Hi, Anna!" calls one of them. "Listen to this guy, will you?"

Anna joins them, and laughs too. They're her friends.

. . . and the Millionaire

Harry Helmsley bought his first building in 1937 for $1,000. Ten years later, he sold it for $165,000. That was just the beginning. Now

Harry owns twenty-seven hotels and 300 office and apartment buildings. He even owns the Empire State Building, one of New York's best-known skyscrapers. He's the tenth wealthiest man in America.

Harry likes to stand at the window of his apartment on the top floor of the Park Lane Hotel, looking out over New York City. He points to one huge building after another.

"I own that one, that one, that one," he says. "I like buying buildings. It's fun."

Harry doesn't look like a tough guy in the New York hotel business. He has white hair, a kind smile, and he looks like a favorite uncle. It's Leona, his wife, who runs the hotel side of the Helmsley empire, and she makes sure that everyone knows she's the boss. Everyone knows how much she loves her husband too. She calls him "Dreamboat," and likes to stand at the piano and sing to him in Harry's Bar in one of their many luxury hotels. For some people, being rich is not enough. They have to be famous too.

Above left:
Homeless in the New York subway
Above right:
Harry Helmsley with his wife, Leona

The Latest Americans

A New Wave

Over 99 percent of all U.S. citizens either came to America from abroad themselves or are the descendants of immigrants. Some were escaping from cruel governments at home, and were looking for freedom to follow their own religion. Many were escaping from hunger and misery on the poor farms and in the great cities of their own countries. Some were brought unwillingly, to work as slaves for American masters. In only one year, 1907, 1.3 million people came to the United States.

Now, at the end of the same century, they have become part of one nation. Most have forgotten their old homes, and can no longer speak their old languages. But now a new wave of immigrants is flowing in. Every year, about 500,000 people are permitted to enter the country. But many more, probably at least another half million, come in secretly, across the 1,936-mile border with Mexico.

A large number of the new immigrants come from South and Central America, especially Mexico. They are usually called "Hispanic," or "Spanish." Some reports say that by the year 2000, over 10 percent of U.S. citizens will be of Latin American origin. But many others are coming from Asia, especially the Philippines, Korea, China, and India.

The Asian newcomers are extraordinarily successful. They make up only 1.6 percent of the nation, but at Harvard, America's oldest and best-known university, 10.9 percent of the new students in 1986 were Asian. And Asian children are winning prizes in schools all over the country.

The United States has also kept its doors open to refugees, people who have had to leave their own countries because of war or because of political problems. There are newly arrived Ethiopians, Iranians, Poles, and Palestinians.

Older Americans have mixed feelings about the newcomers. Many feel that there should be more control over who enters the country.

"Every house needs a door," says Richard Lamm, governor of Colorado, "and every country needs a border." People worry that there will be too many changes, and that there will not be enough jobs for everyone.

On the other hand, most people feel that the United States should go on taking in new people, as it always has done. They realize that new immigrants bring new energy, new hope, and useful skills.

Meanwhile, the new Americans are quietly mixing with the old ones. It's the usual story—what's new and different is more fun than what you've always been used to. So while Mexicans and Chinese are learning to enjoy hot dogs and pizza, their American friends are eating tacos and bird's nest soup. It's all a question of give and take.

Salvador: Across the Rio Grande

Salvador could tell you a great deal about how to build in the local "adobe" style of New Mexico. He knows a lot about it. And everything he knows, he taught himself. He never went to school. On the Mexican ranch where he grew up, the children (Salvador and his twelve brothers and sisters) had to work as hard as the adults.

Once he was grown up and had children of his own, Salvador decided that, somehow, he had to get into the United States. It was just too hard to find a well-paid job in Mexico. Luckily,

The Rio Grande

Salvador outside his home in Alcalde, New Mexico

he had an American brother-in-law, who promised to help him over the border.

With a group of other Mexicans, Salvador set off at night to cross the Rio Grande, the river that divides the United States from Mexico. The water came up to his chest, and he was shaking with cold. He was frightened too. He knew the U.S. Border Patrol was keeping watch on the other bank, waiting to catch the ones who got across. That night, the Mexicans were unlucky. The police caught them.

"Who led you across the river?" they kept on asking. "How much did you pay him? Where were you trying to get to?"

Salvador spent three months in a U.S. prison before he was sent home. But he was not discouraged. For three more months, day and night, he tried to cross the border again. Each time, he heard the border police on the other side and turned back.

In the end, Salvador tried another way. He simply paid a Mexican who was driving into the States to take him too. When they arrived at the crossing point, Salvador pretended to be asleep in the back of the car. The police did not bother to wake him up to ask for his papers. Salvador had arrived in the United States.

At first, Salvador was homesick. But before long, he had made a new life for himself. He married an American, and started a new family. He found work in the building industry. After a couple of years, he managed to get American papers. He became an American citizen himself.

It hasn't always been easy in the States. But Salvador knows how to take care of himself when times are bad. When he's out of work, he collects old aluminum cans and sells them for fifteen cents a pound. These days, though, he isn't out of work very often. Employers don't easily find workers who care so much about their job, and who do it with so much energy and intelligence. They don't want to let him go. In the case of Salvador, it seems as if Mexico has lost and the United States has gained.

Exercises

1 True or false?

1 The American Indians and the Europeans did not have the same feelings about nature.
2 People of many different nationalities have settled in the U.S.A. and have now become the American people.
3 In order to pay for a college education, a young American often does a job which needs very little education.
4 The number of American women who go out to work now is twice what it was in 1950.
5 In the U.S.A. women with young children do not have to stay at home without a job.
6 All Americans agree that life in the U.S.A. is better now than it has ever been.
7 The "typical" American looks forward to "going up in the world."

2 Fill each space with one of the words below.

parent tribes immigrants babies population Europeans citizens Indians

1 Many different .... of .... were living in North America when the first .... arrived.

2 Senior .... often lead a very active life.

3 Fewer .... are being born in the U.S., and the .... is getting older.

4 One in five families in the U.S. is a single-..................... family, and the number continues to rise.

5 Many new .... come from South American and Asian countries.

3 Which of these words and phrases describe the "typical American"?

full of confidence	divorced	busy	proud of being American	unkind to children
hard-working	super intelligent	unfriendly	lazy	unfriendly to immigrants
competitive	independent	easily satisfied		

4 Look at this list of problems in the U.S.A. Which ones have been solved, and which ones are still problems today?

a) giving women the same pay as men for doing the same job
b) stopping drug addiction
c) providing free education for everyone
d) providing medical care which everyone can afford
e) providing jobs for "senior citizens" who do not wish to retire
f) improving the inner cities
g) helping the "underclass" to help themselves
h) providing more rewards for people who work hard

5 Discussion

1 What picture did you have of the "typical American" before you read this chapter? Has this picture changed?
2 Compare the lives of young people/old people/women in the U.S.A. and in your own country.
3 What are the problems of a society where more and more people live beyond the age of sixty-five?

Chapter Two

From the Atlantic to the Pacific

The Grand Canyon

The distance between New York and Hawaii is just about the same as the distance between London and Beijing. No traveler crosses the United States from east to west without being astonished by its size. The airplane speeds on, hour after hour, over rolling farmland, huge cities, empty deserts, high mountains, and wide, fast-flowing rivers.

This is a country without a climate. It has every possible climate. It can snow in New York, be foggy in San Francisco, rain in Atlanta, and be sunny and hot in Phoenix all on the same day. It is a country without one kind of agriculture. It has every kind of agriculture. Anything grows in the hot, wet South. Very little seems to grow in some parts of the cold, windy North.

But America does have one special "way of life." It must have one, because Americans are always talking about it. Perhaps the people you will meet from different parts of the country will tell you what it is...

The Northeast

Old and new buildings in Boston

The raccoon is about the size of a large cat. It is recognized by the black marks on its face and the rings on its tail. It has a strange habit of washing its food before it eats. Raccoons live in woods in most parts of the U.S.A. They are not afraid of humans, and are often found close to large cities.

A Giant Chain of Cities

The U.S. is so enormous that many states are larger than entire countries in Europe. This means that in one region there are great differences of climate and landscape. In the group of states known as the "Northeast," there are mountains, forests, miles of farmland, and some of the largest cities in America.

Two regions make up the Northeast. In the north are the six states of New England: Maine, Vermont, New Hampshire, Massachusetts, Rhode Island, and Connecticut. Further south are the mid Atlantic states: Delaware, Maryland, New Jersey, New York, Pennsylvania, Virginia, West Virginia, and Washington, D.C.

The Northeast is the historic heartland of the U.S., and it is still one of the main centers of population and industry. Once, its factories made textiles, paper, and shoes, but now the Northeast has some of the most advanced modern industry in America. A giant chain of roads, factories, and houses in endless towns and cities runs from Boston right down to Washington, D.C. But even within this huge forest of modern buildings, there are many reminders of the past.

Boston is a city of salty sea air, university professors, and historical streets and houses full of old-fashioned charm. Just across the river, in Cambridge, are Harvard University and the Massachusetts Institute of Technology, two of the greatest centers of education in the U.S., or even in the world.

New York has fewer historical buildings than Boston. But the New Yorkers themselves are the best possible reminders of the human waves of immigrants whose story makes up the modern history of the U.S.A.

Washington, D.C., the seat of government, is quite different again. With its grand architecture, large monuments, and atmosphere of power and politics, Washington is a city to admire rather than to love.

In this climate of extremes, homes and offices are centrally heated in the freezing cold of winter, and air-conditioned in the boiling heat of summer. But man has not quite tamed nature. Raccoons hunt for food in the garbage cans of the suburbs. In the fall, the trees of New England give a magnificent show of golds, reds, and yellows among the white wooden farmhouses. New York State itself has huge forests and wild mountains. Here, away from the cities, it is easy to remember the "land of huge and unknown greatness" found by the first Europeans to arrive in America.

Ellie Archibald of TWA

Only fifty years ago, it was to the great seaports of northeastern America that the millions of new immigrants came. An endless stream of businesspersons, tourists, and other visitors, as well as even more hopeful new Americans still arrive every day. But now they come in huge, silver airplanes, and airports like Logan in Boston are the new gateways to the U.S.

Eleanor ("Ellie") Archibald works at Logan Airport for Trans World Airlines (TWA), one of America's biggest and best-known airlines. She drives to work every day from her apartment in Boston. She's usually at the check-in

desk by 11:00 in the morning, and she works until 8:00 in the evening. It's Ellie's job to greet the hurried, anxious travelers about to leave, and to welcome the more relaxed and cheerful passengers as they arrive.

Ellie has always loved flying. "I had never been on an airplane until I worked for an airline," she says. "Then they sent me on a training flight. So I said to myself, 'This is it. Sink or swim.' And I loved every minute of it."

Working for TWA has given Ellie the chance to travel wherever TWA flies, and that's just about anywhere in the world. She's visited almost every country in Europe, she's been as far west as Bangkok, and as far east as Cairo.

Ellie likes working for TWA. She's well paid, and her coworkers are friendly. But although

her job is interesting, it's not always easy. "You have forty people standing in line," she says, "and they're all in a hurry. They have forty different problems, and you have to help with each one of them. And at the same time, you have to watch out for anything unusual, any bags left lying around. TWA is very, very careful about security."

Ellie has taken French classes to help her with her job. "The United States is such a large country," she says, "and most of us only speak one language. I like meeting foreigners. They've heard so much about Americans. I feel I'm representing America for them." She laughs and shakes the blond hair away from her face. "With the difficult ones, you have to try quite hard to remember that."

Ellie Archibald at Logan Airport, Boston

The Midwest

The "Real" America

The East Coast cities are a "melting pot" of different peoples. But across the Appalachian Mountains in the plains of the Midwest, there is still a strong reminder of Middle Europe. It was here that many Germans, Dutch, Scandinavians, and Eastern Europeans came to live. Now their grandchildren build cars in Detroit, pack meat in Milwaukee, and grow wheat on millions of acres of some of the richest farmland in the world.

Not all midwesterners, of course, have the same origins. Detroit and Chicago have large black populations. In South Dakota, there are still some Sioux Indian villages, and all the cities have their share of the great American national mixture. But the old central European way of life is still remembered by some midwesterners. They celebrate in style with different festivals, like Iowa's July Nordic Fest, or the Dutch Tulip Festival held every May in Pella, near Des Moines.

The Scandinavians and Russians, however, do not need festivals to remind them of their old countries. The winters do that just as well. They are as cold as the winters of Siberia, and wild wolves still live in the forests of Minnesota.

The Midwest is rich in mines and industry, but it is famous for its farms. The earth, said the poet Robert Frost, was good enough to eat. It is certainly good enough to grow food for most of the world. Surprisingly, this is the farmers' problem. The U.S. sells so much of its wheat abroad that the rise and fall of the dollar can change things overnight for the American farmer. When the dollar is low, farmers can sell their wheat abroad for a good price. But when the dollar is high, their wheat is too expensive. As a result of this, many farmers have gone out of business, and there are fewer and fewer small family farms left. Most of them are now huge businesses, employing very few people and using expensive machinery. Many people in the old "Cornbelt" are finding work in industry.

Like their northern European great-grandparents, midwesterners have strong ideas on religion, morals, and politics. Most prefer plain clothes to exciting fashions. They believe in hard work and self-help. The midwesterner, in fact, is often described as the "typical" American. So if you are going to America, forget New York, Disneyland, and the Grand Canyon. Go to Columbus, Ohio. That way you'll see the real thing.

Ivan Sand Down on the Farm

It's lunchtime on the farm. Marjorie Sand rings the big bell outside the door to call her husband, Ivan, and her grandson Harwood in from the cattle shed. There are homemade cookies and apple pie on the table. The old farmhouse is cozy and comfortable. Marjorie made the rag rugs on the floor and the patchwork quilts on the beds, and she collected the antique glass and china on the shelves. She loves pretty things.

Marjorie loves history too. She can tell you all about the country around Riley, Kansas. Over in Wakefield, the farmers were once all English, and in Walsburg they're still mostly Swedish, with their own Swedish church. Ivan's folks were German, but his mom refused to speak the language. "We're Americans now," she used to say. "We're not going to speak German anymore."

Ivan takes off his muddy boots and comes into the kitchen. He was born on this farm, sixty-eight years ago. His father worked 200 acres, with the help of a hired man and a team of horses. Ivan farms 900 acres, with the help of his grandson and $138,000 worth of machinery.

The weather is hard out here in Kansas.

Different kinds of prairie grass once covered much of the Midwest. One of these, called "buffalo grass," grows on the high western plains. It is short and strong and is good for feeding cattle.

The early immigrants from Europe cut out squares of earth and buffalo grass, which has strong roots, and built their houses with them.

Below:
The soya bean harvest
Bottom:
A handful of soya beans

In summer, the temperature rises to 110°F, and by Thanksgiving, in late November, it's snowing. Behind the farmhouse there's a cave in which the family can take shelter if there is a tornado.

But the land is good for farming. It can produce three or four crops of alfalfa a year. And this year has been especially good. Usually, Ivan gets only two or three soya beans in each pod. This year many pods have four beans inside them. But Ivan shakes his head.

"Farmers sell their stuff now for such low prices," he says, "and the cost of fuel and equipment is so high. Our profits are right down. But the fields are lying out there. You've got to keep growing something, and the more you grow, the lower the price you get for it."

Harwood sits down at the table. He's not the same little boy who once put a rubber snake on the step to frighten his grandma. He's a serious young farmer now, his granddad's partner on the farm. He bought twenty-four calves last week that he's feeding up to sell. He'd like to take over the farm one day. But life will have to become a lot easier for American farmers if Harwood is going to keep the farm for as long as his granddad has.

The Rocky Mountains

The Frontier

Mountain lions, or "pumas," are shy animals that almost never attack people. They eat deer, and live in areas where deer can be found. During the day, mountain lions sleep in caves or on sunny rocks. They hunt at night. A male animal can weigh up to 200 pounds, and stands nearly three feet tall at the shoulder.

The early European settlers in America lived on the East Coast. To the west, beyond a line they called the "frontier," the land was full of unknown dangers. The pioneers pushed further and further west until they reached the Pacific Ocean and the frontier was there no longer. But the *idea* of the land beyond the frontier, the land where a man could go and take what he wanted with his skill and courage, had become part of the American dream. The results of this dream can be seen most clearly in the Rockies, the great mass of mountains that runs down the western side of the U.S.

Take Salt Lake City in Utah, for example. It was founded in 1847 by a religious group known as the Mormons. Their leader, Brigham Young, led them on a long journey into the unknown to found a city of their own. "This is the place," he said, when he came through the mountains and first saw the desert valley. Now Salt Lake City is one of the cleanest and best-run cities in the country. The Mormons do not smoke or drink. They lead a strict family life and obey their leaders.

Las Vegas, over the border in Nevada, is very different. Built only for pleasure, the city is the biggest, brightest, richest, meanest casino in the world. The gambling machines work day and night, and you can win or lose a fortune in an hour.

Denver, Colorado, represents a new kind of frontier. Discoveries of oil, gas, coal, and uranium have made it one of the fastest-growing cities in the U.S. But Denver's only water comes from the snow that melts each spring in the high Rockies. Sometimes there is not enough, and the faucets run dry.

Denver's water supply is one of many new problems in the Rockies. The mountains are so enormous that they have always seemed to offer endless supplies of minerals, trees, and wildlife. If you needed more wood, you could cut down another forest. If you wanted water, you could dig another well. Now people are beginning to realize that they must be more careful or they will spoil forever the beauty of their wild places.

Perhaps the loveliest of all these places is the Grand Canyon in Arizona. A mile deep and 217 miles long, even the Grand Canyon is beginning to suffer from too many visitors. Its paths are wearing away, and ugly roads and hotels spoil the view. "It is the one great sight," said President Roosevelt in 1903, "which every American should see." That is the problem. If all Americans come, they will spoil the very wildness and beauty they want to see.

Ranger Dan Davis

"In the East," says Dan Davis, "there's no place you can go where you can't see a fence post, or a house, or a cow. But here, I can look up to the mountains and know that there's nobody for 100 miles."

Dan spends nearly all his time in the mountains, doing the kinds of things he likes best. In the summer, he goes out for days, riding his horse through the back country, sometimes carrying his food and his tent on a llama. In the winter, he skis and builds himself a snow house to sleep in at night. His job, as a ranger in the Rocky Mountains National Park, has taken him into every corner of the huge mountain park.

Dan would like to be the old-fashioned kind of ranger, who spent his time helping people, and telling them where to watch the beavers or look out for mountain lions. But unfortunately, it is also his job to make sure that visitors behave themselves. Every year, the Rocky Mountains park rangers have to deal with 6,000 people breaking the law. Dan's gun is not just part of his uniform. It can be very necessary when he has to arrest a violent person.

The ranger's job has other dangers too. Dan is often called out to rescue people who have gotten themselves into difficulties. It's no fun when the temperature is 30° below zero. "I used to climb myself," says Dan. "Now I've picked up so many dead climbers at the

bottom of cliffs, I don't care to do it anymore. But I worry most about the people who just go off the road and get lost. They can be so foolish, and get into trouble, and then the rangers have the dangerous job of getting them out."

Most of the time, though, Dan loves his work. "There's always something different," he says. "Every day you might be fighting a fire, or trapping an elk, or giving first aid to an injured person."

Dan's father was a park ranger, and as a child, Dan lived in many parks, including the Grand Canyon, Yosemite, the Smoky Mountains, and Glacier. Sometimes he gets restless. He'd like to live in a desert for a while. But Jackie, his wife, loves the mountains and their ranger's cottage, a sixty-year-old log cabin. "I guess we'll have to find a job where we can spend the summer in the mountains and the winter in the desert," says Dan. "But whatever happens, I'll stay in the National Parks Service. I couldn't spend my life just selling shoes in Denver."

Dan Davis in the Rocky Mountains National Park

The Golden State

There are about 30 different kinds of rattlesnakes in North America. They all have the same kind of rattle on the end of their tails, which they shake when danger is near. Rattlesnakes are all poisonous, but with modern medicines few people now die of their bites.

Three great states lie along the Pacific Ocean. Oregon and Washington, to the north, have small populations and many empty spaces, and they are likely to stay that way. Nearly everyone who goes west goes to California.

California is called "the Golden State" after the gold that was found there. But the gold of modern California is the sunshine, which for some people seems just as inviting.

Another kind of gold is the richness of the farmland. The great central valley of California is protected from the Pacific Ocean by mountains all along the coast, and watered by plentiful rivers. It grows enormous quantities of fruit all year round. But California has a more modern harvest than fruit. Silicon Valley, outside San Francisco, is the center of American microtechnology.

Farms and factories need people, and in California a large number of the workers are Hispanic, mainly from Mexico. No one is quite sure how many Mexicans now live in southern California, but they are probably about one-fifth of the population.

To the Mexicans, America is still the land of promise. Some have made money, moved up in the world, and joined the wealthy Californians beside their swimming pools. But many have boring, low-paid jobs as servants and farm and factory workers. When economic troubles come, they are the first to lose their jobs. There is a growing feeling that they, too, want a better share in the good life.

The good life is certainly there in California. It is at its best, perhaps, in San Francisco. This is one of the most beautiful of America's cities with its many hills and flowers, its sea air, and its colorful mixture of nationalities. The good life is less obvious in Los Angeles, a huge city built for the automobile, with its dirty air, endless roads, and uncontrolled building development. Here, more businesses start and fail than anywhere else in the States, and at least one bank is robbed every day.

California has more than its cities. It has the frightening loneliness of Death Valley and the beauty of its forests and mountains. It also has a population that is always looking for something new. California is the place to go if you want to find a new religion, an unusual doctor, or new ideas on anything from food to baby care. It is also, many Americans believe, the place to get rich quick. Not every Californian is rich today, but everyone expects to be rich tomorrow.

Harvest time in California's vineyards

Old style . . .

When David Cootes was a kid, his best friend was Sally the cow. He didn't have much choice up there in the forest above Russian River, in Sonoma County. His school was only one room, with seven or eight children of all ages in it. The teacher had to live with her pupils, moving from one family to the next every few months.

David's other great friend was Ed, his grandfather—when he wasn't drinking. Ed taught him to trap and skin wild animals. He was a real old mountain man, always ready for a gunfight or a poker game. There were just a few people around then, still living in the goldminers' and woodcutters' cabins. David remembers them all.

"Old Billy saw a rattlesnake going under his cabin, so he picked it up and threw it over his shoulder. Billy didn't know it, but Bruce was just behind him, and the snake wrapped itself around Bruce's neck. Well, Bruce got free somehow, but then he went after Billy with his gun. He never got him though."

David sounds a little regretful. He's a successful insurance man now in San Francisco and he only comes out to the old house on weekends. But give him a hat and a pair of guns, and he wouldn't look too different from an oldtimer himself . . .

. . . and new style

By the year 2000, claims the United Nations, the ten largest cities on earth will be on the Pacific. The West Coast of the U.S. is proving already that the Pacific is the ocean of the future. In its big cities, the numbers of people from Korea, Samoa, Taiwan, the Philippines, and Vietnam are growing all the time. Ten years ago, mailboxes in San Francisco carried names like Goldschmidt, Fellini, O'Riley, and Dickson. Now the names are Wong, Chung, Morikawa, and Truang.

One new arrival is Raymond Guevarra. He came to San Francisco eighteen months ago from the Philippines. He started as a salesperson in a radio store, but he soon became the store manager. It's not surprising. Raymond is not only friendly with the customers, he's well qualified too. He has a master's degree in engineering, and he left a good job in the Philippines to come to the U.S.

"I'm aiming high," says Raymond. "I want to have my own business one day. I think it's more interesting to work really hard and get what you want in life."

Raymond certainly knows about hard work. He's on the job for ten hours a day, six days a week. If he goes on like this, he'll get where he wants to be soon enough. Let's just hope he finds it has all been worth it.

Below:
David Cootes at his home in Sonoma County, California
Bottom:
Raymond Guevarra at work in San Francisco

The Southwest

New Mexico and Texas

Giant cactus plants in the southwestern U.S. can grow up to 16 feet high. They do not flower until they are over 50 years old, and they die at about 150 or 200 years of age. The red fruits are collected and eaten.

It's easy to say where one state in the U.S.A. ends and another begins. You need only look at the lines on the map. It's not so easy to say where one region ends and another begins. The Southwest region, for example, usually means Texas and the neighboring states, Arkansas, Oklahoma, and New Mexico. But Arkansas is in some ways a typically southern state, with its cotton plantations and rice fields. Oklahoma's rich farmland seems to belong with its northern neighbors. New Mexico is, as its name suggests, strongly Mexican in flavor. And Texas is so big and so different that it's almost a region in itself.

The size of Texas is something that visitors cannot get used to. Three times the size of Great Britain, and bigger than France, it raises more cattle, grows more peanuts, and harvests more fruit than any other state.

For a long time, Texas has been the state where everything is possible. Huge fortunes have been made in oil, farming, and industry. In spite of the heat coming off those flat, dusty plains life is comfortable for those who can afford air-conditioning. And most people can. The people of Houston, one of Texas's largest cities, pay over $700 million a year just to cool off their houses.

Further west, in New Mexico, the land rises, and the scenery becomes more exciting. Rivers cut into the rock, making deep valleys, and the Sandia Mountains rise up to a height of nearly 11,000 feet. From the top you can see for hundreds of miles. In the north is Santa Fe, with its lovely old "adobe" houses, made of mud bricks. In the south is Indian country, a huge, dry, beautiful land, almost empty of people. Indians have lived here for thousands of years, and some of their ancient villages can still be seen.

The Southwest is changing faster than any other part of the U.S. with its growing numbers of "Mexamericans." These new immigrants, unlike earlier ones, are not in a hurry to forget their own language. In some areas, such as the Rio Grande valley, 90 percent of the people are Spanish speakers.

The language question has caused a lot of discussion in the States. Should every American speak English, or should two languages be allowed side by side? Whoever wins the argument, one thing is certain. You'll need to bring your Spanish dictionary if you travel in the Southwest for many years to come.

Henry McKinley—Rancher

Henry McKinley enjoys watching cowboy movies. He has fun seeing the things they do wrong. "For one thing," he says, "we don't get all that fighting anymore. If you have a disagreement with someone, you go to a lawyer."

Henry knows what he's talking about. He was raised on a ranch himself. He rode his first bucking calf when he was four years old. Ghost Ranch, where he spent his childhood, didn't only raise cattle; it took in visitors as well. Henry can remember when Cary Grant and John Wayne came to stay.

College and then the army took Henry away from home. But he took his rope with him when he went off to be a soldier, and even in Korea and Hawaii he found horses to ride and cattle to rope.

Henry has spent most of his working life out in the open, employed by the Bureau of Land Management and the Bureau of Indian Affairs. But in his spare time he went on training horses and teaching kids to work with them too. He got more pleasure from teaching a deaf child to rope a wild horse than from the many prizes he has won for his own rodeo skills.

Training a horse, Henry says, is a long job. "You rope him, you tie up one foot, then you hit him all over with a sack until he stops jumping about. Then you put the saddle on, and a noseband. You tie that to the tail, and it teaches him to turn. When he's turning real well, you can ride him in a corral. Then you

Left:
Henry McKinley on his ranch near Santa Fe, New Mexico
Above:
Detail of gloves, ropes, and saddle

can take him outside. Two years later you might have a good horse, if you work him every day."

Henry and his wife, Peggy, work full-time now on their own ranch near Santa Fe, New Mexico. It isn't always easy. There's so little rain that Henry can only keep 300 cattle on his 30,000-acre ranch. Snakeweed is a danger. A cow that eats it can lose her unborn calf. Cattle thieves are a problem too. They can bring up a cattle truck, fill it with cows, and drive off while Henry is miles away on the other side of his ranch, mending a fence.

But the good times make up for the bad times. As the sun rises, Henry is out on his horse, looking across the misty miles to the Sangre de Cristo Mountains. "That's my religion," he says. "The sun, the grass, the mountains, and the morning."

The South

New Days, New Ways

Below:
The "Old South"—a nineteenth-century plantation house in Natchez, Mississippi
Bottom:
The "New South"—the Peachtree Center, Atlanta, Georgia

The Mississippi alligator lives in rivers, lakes, and marshes between Texas and North Carolina. Alligators were once common in the South, but they were hunted for their fine skins, and many baby alligators were sold as pets. People are now no longer allowed to hunt or trap alligators without a special license, and the numbers are growing again.

If you drive south from the huge, busy cities of the eastern states, you will see the country around you slowly changing. As you go through North Carolina, South Carolina, and on into Georgia, the air becomes heavier, the trees greener, and the country more tropical. You will find old-fashioned politeness and a quieter, slower way of talking. And you will find more Bibles and more guns than in other parts of the country.

Throughout American history, the southern states have been different from the North. The warm climate and great rivers made it easy to grow cotton. Black slaves were brought from Africa to work in the fields, and for 200 years "King Cotton" ruled in the South.

In 1861 a bitter war broke out between the northerners, who wanted to end slavery, and the southerners, who wanted to keep their slaves. The war ended in 1865, but it took many years for the South to recover. Black slaves were freed, but their lives were still hard. In some states, right up until 1965, blacks could not go to "white" schools, eat in "white" restaurants, or even make a call from a "white" public phone booth. But then came the Civil Rights movement, led by Martin Luther King, Jr., and at last, changes began to come.

Change came, in fact, with extraordinary speed. There are still poor blacks in unhealthy black housing, blacks still die younger, have low-paid jobs, and are the most often unemployed. But there are now black mayors, black doctors and lawyers, and black students at the best universities. As a black preacher said, "We ain't [*aren't*] what we ought to be, we ain't what we're going to be. But, thank the Lord God Almighty, we ain't what we was."

In other ways, too, the South has changed. "King Cotton" is no longer all powerful. Industries of all kinds are growing rapidly in the South. The South, in fact, is the fastest-growing region of the U.S. today. But in spite of this, the "Old South" has managed to keep some of its beauty and charm. The fascinating streets of New Orleans, and the lovely old houses of towns like Savannah, Georgia, still bring back memories of days long gone.

Old days and old ways may change, but the weather never will. The warmth of the "Sunbelt" has persuaded many retired people to leave the northern "Snowbelt" and spend their last years in comfort. So if you ever go to Florida, take everything with you. You may decide to stay there for the rest of your life.

Angelique Jordan— At the Top of Her Class

At sixteen, Angelique Jordan was at the top of her class. Now, at thirty-two, she's still at school. Only this time she's the teacher, not the student.

"Maybe I could have been a singer or a model," she says, with just a little regret in her voice. "But when I was a kid, the people I admired and looked up to were teachers, so here I am teaching."

There was one teacher she admired more than all the others. His name was Bob Jordan, and when Angelique had finally grown up and finished her college education, she married him.

Like many black southerners in the 1960s, Bob Jordan joined the Civil Rights movement. He marched with Martin Luther King, took part in demonstrations, and was even sent to jail. It was worth the struggle.

"Many of the things I'm able to do now I was not able to do earlier," says Angelique. "I can eat anywhere I want to eat, I can go anywhere I want to go. It's not the same as the 1950s."

Angelique's little girl, Kelly, is enjoying a childhood very different from her mother's. Angelique and her six brothers and sisters lived in a small, overcrowded apartment. Kelly has a beautiful big house and yard in a lovely suburb of Atlanta to run around in. When Angelique was a little girl, she used to walk along the street where she now lives and admire the lovely homes in it. No black people lived in the neighborhood then. She never imagined that one day she'd be living there herself.

But the Jordan family is too busy to spend much time at home. Angelique starts the day at 5:00 every morning, when she cleans the house and does her exercises. Then she joins a carpool (a group of several people sharing one car) to get to work, and is busy all day in the classroom. She's home again by 3:45, and picks Kelly up from her sister-in-law, who looks after her during the day. Then mother and daughter read, draw, paint, and watch TV together.

"Kelly's only three, but she knows so much already," says Angelique proudly. "She knows how to spell her name, she knows her address and her phone number, she knows all the streets around here."

She goes over to the beautiful toy kitchen, where Kelly is pretending to fry a plastic steak on a plastic stove for her momma, and picks her little daughter up.

"Just think, I didn't go on a plane till I was in twelfth grade. Kelly flew when she was only six months old."

Angelique Jordan at the end of the school day

Exercises

1 Match the description with the region, state, or city.

1 The Northeast	a) Rich in oil, changing faster than any other part of the U.S.A., and with a language problem.
2 The Midwest	b) Famous as a centre of learning.
3 The Rockies	c) Famous for cotton, but new industries are growing fast.
4 The Southwest	d) A city where the central government offices are.
5 The South	e) The state that raises the most cattle.
6 Boston, Massachusetts	f) Once famous for gold, but now for its fruit, new technology, and new ideas.
7 Texas	g) It could produce enough food to feed most of the world, but also has industries.
8 Columbus, Ohio	h) A natural dividing line between east and west.
9 Washington, D.C.	i) Where Europeans first began to settle, and where a large percentage of Americans still live.
10 California	j) A city where you'll find more "typical Americans" than in New York.

2 Copy the chart below on a large piece of paper.
Write the following states in the correct column.

Arizona, Arkansas, California, Colorado, Connecticut, Delaware, Florida, Georgia, Iowa, Kansas, Maine, Maryland, Massachusetts, Minnesota, Nevada, New Hampshire, New Jersey, New Mexico, New York, North Carolina, Ohio, Oklahoma, Oregon, Pennsylvania, Rhode Island, South Carolina, Texas, Utah, Vermont, Virginia, Washington, West Virginia.

Northeast	Midwest	Rockies	West Coast	Southwest	South

If you know the names of any other states, write them into the chart also.

3 Fill each space with one of the words given below.

central   different   historical   immigrants   same   natural

1 Boston is one of the most . . . . cities in the U.S.A.

2 Most of America's first . . . . arrived by sea.

3 The Midwest is where large numbers of people from . . . . and northern Europe settled.

4 In America, the climate is . . . . from region to region, and the day's weather in different parts of the

   country is never the . . . .

5 The Grand Canyon is a place of . . . . beauty which could easily be spoiled by too many visitors.

4 Discussion

1 If you could visit only one of the six regions of the U.S.A., which would you choose? Why?

2 Why do people think that Midwesterners are "typical" Americans?

3 What are the advantages if everyone in the U.S.A. speaks English as their first language? Do you see any disadvantages?

4 "We ain't what we ought to be, we ain't what we're going to be. But, thank the Lord God Almighty, we ain't what we was." What was this Southern preacher's vision of the past, present, and future of black people in the U.S.A.?

Chapter Three

American Institutions

The White House, Washington, D.C.

Americans talk with pride of their government and institutions. They seem certain that they have more freedom, better laws, stronger leaders, and more open, honest newspapers than anywhere else in the world. But even the most patriotic Americans have a few doubts. Education is one problem area, and so is the law. There are not enough clever teachers, and too many clever lawyers.

Americans feel confident that they know what is going on, and that they can change things that don't work. A bad President can be voted out. A bad doctor can be taken to court. A bad soldier can be punished. It may be this that gives them so much confidence in their system. Of course things go wrong, as they do everywhere else in the world, but at least people feel that they can do something about it.

Government

Wave the flag, Mr. President

Americans are not afraid to show how they feel, and when the feeling is patriotism, they get up and shout about it. They like to read and hear about the heroes of American history. They enjoy patriotic songs like "America the Beautiful." And the sight of their flag on important national occasions can bring tears to their eyes.

Americans want to be proud of their President, as well as their country. They like him to be good-looking, religious, and a good family man. They want him to be strong, to be a good talker, and to be confident about the future. They expect him to keep the prices down at home and to keep the country looking powerful abroad.

A President has to make his job look easy, and smile confidently when he speaks to the nation on TV. But in fact, his job is an impossible one. He cannot do as much as he would like, or as the country expects him to do. He can make decisions, but he cannot always persuade people to carry them out. President Truman once said that getting anything done from the White House was like "pushing a damp noodle across a table."

One of the President's biggest difficulties is that every decision he makes must also be approved by Congress. But Congress can, and quite often does, refuse to give its approval. A President who knows how to get Congress on his side is likely to be a successful President.

The United States government is of course more than the President and the Congress. It employs over 18,000,000 people. Many Americans think there are far too many of them. "Don't go by train," they will tell you. "The railroad's no good. It's run by the government." It's not really surprising that so many people dislike government control. After all, many of their grandparents came to the States to get away from powerful governments, at home.

Dislike of government power doesn't stop people from feeling patriotic though. It certainly didn't stop the Californian who invented a flag-waving machine, so that people could show their feelings without getting tired.

Senator Grassley of Iowa

Smart politicians in Washington still laugh at Senator Grassley. They are not used to seeing a senator with the hands of a working man, who talks like a farmer.

"What's the price of a cow in Iowa, Chuck?" asks one, as they pass each other on the way to vote in the Senate Chamber.

"How are your pigs doing, Senator?" asks another, smiling.

They are right about one thing. Senator Grassley is a farmer. He was born on a farm in Iowa, and he and his wife, Barbara, raised five children on their own 240-acre farm. And at weekends, when other senators are playing golf or tennis, Chuck Grassley is at home, cleaning out his pigpen or planting next year's corn.

The politicians are wrong about the rest. Senator Grassley is not dumb. He's intelligent, in a way that Washington understands. When he takes hold of an idea, he won't let it go. He's like a dog that has caught a rat. The Pentagon, which controls America's spending on defense, has learned to dislike Senator Grassley. He has shown how much money is wasted by the military—money that is needed, for example, by the farmers of Iowa.

Those Iowan farmers recognize Chuck Grassley as one of themselves. They like his plain, no-nonsense way of speaking. They like his honesty. They like the way he is always ready to see them in his office, anytime they come to Washington. Many of them, like him, are old-fashioned Christians, for whom the Bible is a book of instructions. Like him, they hate communism. Most of them have never visited another country, but they are still sure that Americans enjoy more freedom than any other nation on earth.

To keep their support, Grassley visits every one of the ninety-nine counties of Iowa each year. It takes endless time and energy.

"I don't know how he does it," says one of Grassley's assistants. "He seems to have a couple of extra batteries."

Chuck Grassley has had to pay a price for his success. "If there's any one regret, it is that I have not spent enough time with my kids," he says. "My family has always come second to my public life. I'm not sure if that's right, but that's a fact."

Senator Grassley on the steps of the Capitol, Washington, D.C.

Hawks and Doves

"We need more fighter planes, more submarines, more missiles," say the chiefs of the U.S. army, navy, and air force. From their offices in the Pentagon, the huge, five-sided Department of Defense in Washington, the message comes across loud and clear. Defense spending must continue to increase. Congress must continue to pay the bills.

Some politicians are happy to pay. They want the U.S. to be the strongest nation in the world whatever it costs. They are afraid of the strength of the Soviet Union, of the weakness of friendly countries in Europe, and of communism everywhere. They are known as "hawks."

Other politicians are worried by how much money disappears every year into the Department of Defense. When one submarine costs well over $100 million, they feel the government should think twice about buying another. They are worried by the dangers of the arms race, and by reports of waste and bad management in the armed forces. At the same time, they believe that it is better to find answers to problems by diplomacy, not by war. These politicians are known as "doves."

When the talk is all about submarines, nuclear missiles, and weapons in space, it is easy to forget the ordinary soldier, sailor, marine, and airman. But in fact, there are over two million of them, half of whom are stationed outside the U.S.

Americans are glad to know that they are there. They like to feel that their country is respected by the rest of the world, and they are afraid of appearing weak. They like a President who takes strong action to protect Americans abroad. But at the same time, Americans do not like to see their soldiers actually fighting. The Vietnam War is still a painful memory for many people.

Some nations make heroes of their soldiers and sailors, and love to see them march in colorful uniforms. But American soldiers usually stay out of sight on great public occasions. The parades on the Fourth of July, the U.S.A.'s independence day, are organized by the town, not by the army. After all, life in the army is a serious business. It is at its most serious, perhaps, at West Point Academy, where young officers are trained. The aim of West Point, said one general, "is to put iron in your soul." Perhaps it is not surprising that almost one-third of the cadets never manage to finish the program.

Alex Feliciano of the U.S. Marines

It takes weeks of training, days of getting up at 4 A.M., hours of marching, and miles of running to become a marine. But it takes a childhood in Puerto Rico, a lifelong love of the United States, and a lot of ambition to become a marine like Alex Feliciano.

To Alex, being a marine is the best thing in the world. When he's guarding the American Embassy in a foreign country, the eyes under that white cap are shining with pride.

"When a kid looks at you, he wonders who you are, and how tough your training is. And he's thinking, 'What has that guy done? Could I do it too?' I like to see the small kids look at me that way. I feel so proud to belong to the United States, which is one of the greatest countries in the world at any time in history. And to be a marine, which is the best fighting force in the world. I know those kids look at me and want to be where I am."

Alex has been in several foreign countries. He went first to Iwakuni, Japan. "I went to see Hiroshima and the peace park. I saw what can actually happen to a country when it is involved in a nuclear war. It was extraordinary how friendly the Japanese were to us, after something like that happened."

Alex saw a more modern war in Beirut, Lebanon. He was guarding the American Embassy when it was attacked by rockets and gunfire.

"I felt a little fear, but I thought about my training and my duties as a marine. We had to protect the embassy and the Americans who worked there. The worst thing was we were afraid of being caught, and becoming hostages. But we got out all right."

Costa Rica, Alex's next post, was much more peaceful. It was one he'll never forget, because he met a beautiful girl one day in the embassy, when he went to pick up some mail. He asked someone who she was, and managed to meet her again. They got married a year later.

Alex is back in the U.S. now, at Quantico, Virginia, not far from Washington, D.C. It's rather dull after all his adventures abroad, but there's a lot of excitement at home. His first child, baby Alex, is just a few weeks old. Daddy has his future planned for him already.

"I always wanted to be a pilot on military aircraft," says Alex, "and I would like him to fulfill my dream."

No doubt baby Alex will soon have his first toy airplane. It's never too soon to start training.

Above:
Alex Feliciano on duty in Quantico, Virginia
Left:
Alex in his dress uniform (the "Blues")

Law and Order

Half a Million Lawyers

"It was you, wasn't it?" says the district attorney, pointing to the woman on the other side of the courtroom. "It was you who murdered your husband."

"Yes!" says the woman, hiding her face in her hands. "Oh God, yes, it was me!"

"OK. Cut!" shouts the movie director. "One minute break, everyone." He is pleased. He knows that his TV series will be a success. The great interest that Americans have in the law and the courts will make sure of that.

It is extraordinary, in fact, how important the law is in America's national life. Indeed, the justices of the Supreme Court are some of the most powerful people in America. It is often they, rather than the politicians, who make the big decisions that will change people's daily lives. It is the justices who decide that black children and white children should go to school together. It is they who decide whether criminals should be punished by death. Politicians, after all, can lose an election if they make unpopular decisions. Justices keep their job for life.

The nine justices of the Supreme Court are probably the most respected people in the U.S.A., but Americans do not think so highly of the less important lawyers. Perhaps this is because there are so many of them. One in every 450 Americans is a lawyer, and in Washington, D.C., the number is one in every sixty-four.

One reason for the large number of lawyers is that each state has different laws. In Alabama, for example, the school age is from seven to sixteen years old. In Pennsylvania, it is eight to seventeen. In addition to the different state laws, there are also federal laws, which everyone must obey.

Americans hurry to the courts of law to fight for their rights for all kinds of reasons. This can be a good thing. No employer can afford to be careless about safety. The workers might take him to court. No doctor can be careless with her patient. She will find herself in court, ordered to pay millions of dollars for her mistake.

Some people feel that things have gone too far. Take Mr. and Mrs. Zak, for example. One evening they offered scotch to a guest who then drove off in his car and crashed. The court decided that the Zaks had been wrong to give their guest scotch and allow him to drive away drunk. They were ordered to pay $72,500. It must have been the most expensive bottle of scotch the Zaks ever bought.

Bill Napolitano— A New York City Cop

Bill Napolitano's police uniform is more than just a shirt, slacks, and a cap. He also has to carry a radio, two pairs of handcuffs, a flashlight, a set of keys, a notebook, a heavy stick, and a .38 Smith and Wesson gun. You might think that the gun is the most important item. But Bill has been a New York City cop for three years, and he hasn't used it once. In fact, it's his notebook that he needs most often.

"There's a lot of paperwork involved in what we do," says Bill. We have to write reports on everything—complaints, parking offenses, burglaries—it's very boring."

Sometimes, though, Bill's job is anything but boring. A few weeks ago, a New York police officer was shot and killed by a drug addict. During the funeral, a woman called the police station. She said that she had seen a man on the balcony of her apartment trying to force his way in.

"My partner, Tom, was at the funeral," remembers Bill, "so I drove the sergeant there. We went up on the roof and searched it. There are small areas up there on the rooftops, fenced in, where people have barbecues and so on. The sergeant saw the guy, but he ran away. So we chased him, and he jumped off the side of the building onto a terrace and swung himself down onto the floor below. We got him on the third floor, and he tried to run but we stopped him. I looked in his jacket and found a gun. He looked just like the guy who murdered the police officer. My heart was

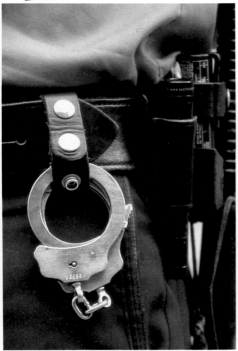

going fast, I can tell you! Later, we found out he wasn't the murderer, but he had a long record of robbery and violence."

Bill has seen a change in crime since he became a cop. New, dangerous drugs have spread like wildfire through the city, and addicts rob and steal to get the money to pay for them.

Most calls to the police station, though, are the same as they have always been. People hear screams from a family fight going on in the next apartment, and they call the cops.

"You have to go in and settle things fast," says Bill. "Sometimes you go to a place, and the people don't have much money, and maybe the father's out of work, and he's drinking, or on drugs, or it might be the mother. And it's terrible because of the children. The children have nowhere to go. They don't know where to go."

Above right:
Bill Napolitano on duty in New York City
Above left:
Bill's name and number on his uniform shirt
Below left:
Some of Bill's equipment

Education

A Process that Never Stops

There are 226,500,000 Americans, and nearly 60,000,000 of them go to school. This very high percentage includes five-year-old Marlene Vogel at her kindergarten, and seventeen-year-old Leroy Washington at his high school. It also includes forty-three-year-old Hymie Cohen, who is taking a part-time course in car maintenance.

Americans have always believed in education, but in a specially American way. The schools' first job was to turn millions of foreign children into Americans. Since they came from dozens of different countries, this was not easy. Schools had to teach the children to speak English, to love their new country, and to learn how to live in it. American schools were the "melting pot" in which the differences were forgotten. They were the ladder up which the poor could climb to a better life. Getting started on a successful career was the main aim. Most American parents still care less for book-learning than for a practical education that will help their child to find a job.

In trying to make children equal, American schools do not always encourage the smartest children to do their best. This means that many middle-class people, who want their children to be highly educated, send them off to private schools. At the same time, there is a growing difference between public schools in rich areas and those in poorer areas. Mississippi, for example, spends $1,300 a year on each student. Massachusetts, a much richer state, spends $2,400. The differences between good schools and bad schools are getting greater all the time.

Many Americans are worried about their public schools. They see serious problems of violence, and failure. They see too many children who never learn to read or write properly, too few college graduates who can speak a foreign language, and too many teachers who cannot spell.

But it is easy to forget the great successes of American education. Its best universities are among the best anywhere. American philosophers and economists are world-famous, and American scientists win more than their share of Nobel prizes. But perhaps most important of all is that American education never stops. If seventy-two-year-old Myra Katzman wants to learn creative story-writing, or Italian art, or chess, she can go to her nearest college and take a course in it. And millions of Myras are doing just that.

Children going home in a school bus

Abby and Eliza Davis— Schoolgirls

Like many sisters, Abby and Eliza Davis couldn't be more different. Twelve-year-old Eliza is full of energy, and always has something to say. Nine-year-old Abby is quieter. She's happiest when she has a good book to read. Eliza wants to be a lawyer or a clothes designer one day. She just can't wait to grow up and go away to college. Abby wants to be a doctor when she grows up. She works hard at math and science, her favorite subjects.

Eliza is in the seventh grade, and has just started at junior high school. She gets up every day at 5:30, to wash and blowdry her hair. She's ready to leave the house at 6:50, to meet her friends by the store for a snack. The kids have a mile and a half to walk to school, and the bell rings at 7:30. If you aren't in your place by 7:45, you're in trouble.

At 11:20, the children have their lunch. Some children eat the hot dog, chicken pot pie, or steak sandwich that the school provides, but Eliza prefers to bring her own lunch in a lunchbox. At 2:15, classes are finished and it's time for sports. Eliza usually has hockey practice until 4:30. She's tired by the time her mother comes to get her in the car, but she still has two or three hours of homework to do before she goes to bed.

Abby is in the fourth grade at Broken Ground School. She's lucky. Her school has big modern classrooms, first-class teachers, and an excellent library. The playground is surrounded by beautiful woods, where Indians once camped. The problems of America's big-city public schools seem a long way away from New Hampshire.

Like many American schoolchildren, Abby starts the day by saluting the American flag, the "stars and stripes," which hangs in her classroom, and repeating the words of the pledge of allegiance. Then work begins. Today, she's writing a composition about her summer vacation. Her pencil moves busily across the paper.

"We're here! Boy, is it hot! I got some cookies and ice cream in the airport. We're fishing right now. My dad caught one fish and Eliza got the fishhook caught in her finger..."

Abby will finish her story at home this evening, while Eliza does her homework. Will they work together peacefully, or will they fight?

"Well," says Abby, "we have arguments, but we get along pretty well. About fifty-fifty, I'd say."

That's not bad for two such different sisters.

Below:
Eliza (left) with her friends on the way to school
Bottom:
Abby at work in the classroom

Religion

In God We Trust

In Garden Grove, California, people arrive at the Crystal Cathedral, a huge glass church built at the cost of $18 million. Helpers in gold jackets show them where to park their cars. As the service begins, doors ninety feet high open, showing twelve fountains, one for each of the first followers of Christ. As the service continues, enormous television screens appear, so that those in the back can see the preacher's face. Caged birds sing, and cameras click.

The Reverend Robert Schuller, who opened the Crystal Cathedral in 1980, is one of a new kind of religious leader. Schuller, like the others, runs Christian TV shows, which are watched by millions of viewers. The shows are full of religious emotion, with lively music and stories of people whose lives have been changed through prayer.

Preachers like Schuller are extraordinarily popular, especially in the southern states, the most religious region of the U.S. They own many TV and radio stations, known as the "electronic church." They persuade their viewers to give millions of dollars a year. Jerry Falwell, one of the best known, raises at least $50 million a year, and is building an entire Christian university with some of the money. Most of these preachers speak out strongly against communists, Roman Catholics, and equal rights for women. Some believe the poor should not receive help from the government, but should learn to help themselves.

This new kind of Evangelical Christian leader worries the older churches, both Protestant and Catholic. They don't like the mixture of money, politics, religion, and emotion. They believe that religion is a question of faith, and of showing the love of God to others. They work hard in their smaller, local churches, and give generously to the needy. But their churches usually remain the same size, while the new kind of Evangelical churches grow.

Christianity, of course, is not the only religion in the U.S. There are increasing numbers of Muslims and Buddhists. There are also about six million Jews, who do not all pray in the same way, but who do agree that America should remain a friend of Israel. America also has many unusual religions: Indian gurus, faith healers, and "saints" with strange ideas.

Religion is a very important part of life in the U.S. Over 90 percent of Americans say they believe in God. Over 40 percent go to a church or synagogue at least once a week. Even their money reminds them of religion. The words "In God We Trust" are stamped on the coins.

> Nearly 25% of the U.S. population is Roman Catholic, and six million are Jewish. But 90% of all the churches are Protestant. There are many different Protestant groups, including Baptists, Methodists, and Lutherans. Some religions, like the Mormons and the Jehovah's Witnesses, were founded in the U.S.A.

Dr. Joel Gregory of the Southern Baptist Church

Like all true Texans, Dr. Joel Gregory likes talking about size. He likes to remind you, for example, that the Southern Baptist Church, with sixteen million members, is the largest Protestant group in the U.S. Travis Road Baptist Church, where Dr. Gregory is the pastor, is the largest church in Fort Worth, Texas. And the Southwestern Baptist College, where Dr. Gregory spent five years as Professor of Preaching, is the largest theological college in the entire history of world Christianity.

Also, like all true Texans Joel Gregory has no desire to live anywhere but Texas. The last pastor at Travis Road stayed in the job for twenty-three years. Joel Gregory would like to do the same. The job is big enough to keep

Left:
*Travis Road Baptist Church,
Fort Worth, Texas*
Above:
*Dr. Joel Gregory and his
family*

him busy for at least that long. With 7,000 members, the church employs ten full-time ministers, and spends $2,275,000 a year. "I need to be a good manager," says Dr. Gregory with a smile.

At least Joel Gregory has had plenty of experience. He took over his first church when he was only nineteen, just married, and still a student. It was a small church in the inner city, where violence was common. The young pastor had to cope with everything—performing weddings and funerals, preaching, and advising all who came to him. At the same time, he was studying first for his master's degree, then for a Ph.D.

Life is not much less busy now. Take an average Sunday, for example. It starts at 6:30 A.M. when Dr. Gregory works out the final details of his sermon on his computer. After

two hours of prayer and Bible study, he goes to his church, where Sunday school (for 2,000 students) starts at 9:30. Before the main service begins at 11:00, a makeup artist prepares his face for the TV cameras. Up to 50,000 people will watch the service and listen to the thirty-minute sermon, in their own homes.

Lunch with family and guests at a dinner club follows. Then after a short rest, there will be one meeting after another until the evening service starts at 7:00 P.M. And even after that, there will be more meetings for the young people.

Meetings, meetings, meetings—the story of Joel Gregory's life. "You know what they say in Texas," he says. "The government builds the roads, and the Baptists wear them out going to meetings."

The Media

Soap Operas and News Shows

The news may be full of man-made wars and natural disasters, but many Americans are more interested in other matters. How is their favorite cop planning to catch his next criminal? How will beautiful Sally-Ann get out of the trouble she has gotten herself into? To their audiences, the characters in the weekly TV serial shows (known as soap operas) have become more important than real people.

Television has an enormous effect on Americans. Politicians know all about this. They try to make their big public speeches at times when they can get the largest audiences on the evening news programs. Advertisers, too, understand the power of television. They are willing to spend billions of dollars a year on television advertising. After all, the average American

TV reporters interview a politician outside the Capitol in Washington, D.C.

watches TV for thirty hours a week. By the age of eighteen, an American child will have spent between 15,000 and 18,000 hours in front of the television, and only 11,000 hours in school.

The strange thing is that neither politicians nor advertisers like to admit that watching violence on TV leads to greater violence on the streets.

"There is no real proof," they say, and the blood on the screen continues to flow.

Many people admit that the quality of television could be better. They would prefer to see fewer soap operas and crime series, and more history, drama, and science. One reason for the poor quality is that the TV companies make most of their money by selling advertising. Advertisers pay more money for time during popular shows, especially in the evenings when the audiences are biggest.

"If we show serious programs," say the TV companies, "the advertisements will look meaningless, and that won't please the advertisers."

The news about American television is not all bad. For one thing, Americans themselves are turning off the more violent shows, and watching more comedy and news programs. For another, the news programs themselves are becoming more interesting. The most popular is "60 Minutes." If you haven't watched it on Sunday, you won't know what your friends are talking about on Monday, Tuesday, and Wednesday.

The last word, of course, is always with the audience. If they don't like what they see, they can turn off the TV. Elvis Presley, the late king of rock, had a better idea. He once became so angry with what he was watching that he grabbed his gun and shot the TV set. Who says that watching television doesn't lead to violence?

Grace Diekhaus of 60 Minutes

You've just finished high school, you want more than anything else to be an actress, and your parents want you to learn to type instead. What do you do? Grace Diekhaus decided to please her parents, but the job she found was as near to films and acting as she could get. She became a secretary at CBS, one of America's most important TV companies.

"I wanted to work in the drama department, but they sent me to the newsroom," says Grace. "Five minutes later, I knew I wanted to

be a journalist. The atmosphere, the excitement—I loved it. I never, ever gave acting another thought."

Grace still loves it. She's working now for "60 Minutes," the news program that's been in the top ten American TV shows for the last ten years. She's a producer. That means she has to put together and film the kind of fifteen-minute news stories that make up the program.

Grace has just finished a piece on why Asian children are doing so well in American schools. She worked with a Vietnamese assistant, who contacted the parents and children. Then she went to California, and filmed children at school and at home. They were interviewed by Mike Wallace, one of the show's presenters, and finally Grace went through the film to shape it into a finished piece.

When you do your job as well as Grace does hers, you can laugh at the few mistakes you've made. She remembers the time she worked on a program about Ronald Reagan before he became president.

"The last part of the piece was a film of Ronald Reagan announcing that he was going to try for the presidency. So the Reagans came out to the microphones, and there were hundreds of journalists there. Our "60 Minute" team was the most important team there, right in the middle, and I said, "Roll it!" to the cameraman, so he began to film. And I felt something on my foot, like spaghetti, but I was so interested in watching the Reagans, I didn't look down. And when he'd finished making the announcement, I looked down and my feet were all covered in tape. The sound man hadn't put the tape onto the machine properly. There we were, a million-dollar team, up in front of everyone, and we lost the whole interview!"

Grace doesn't often lose an interview, but she does often lose a weekend. She travels so much for her job that she seldom has time to spend at her weekend home with her husband, Peter Levinson. And even when she does have time off, you can guess what she does. That's right. She watches television.

There are hundreds of small TV stations in the U.S.A., but there are three main companies, called *networks*, that broadcast to the whole country. These are:

CBS (Columbia Broadcasting Service)

ABC (American Broadcasting Company)

NBC (National Broadcasting Company)

Grace Diekhaus at her home in Manhattan

Paying the Price

Louis Bonesio was fifty-one when he went into the hospital for a new heart. By the age of sixty-two, he also had two new hips made of steel, and was back in hospital to get a new kidney. Three weeks later he was at home once more, ready to carry on with his usual hobbies: motorcycling, fishing, and hot-air ballooning.

For people like Louis Bonesio, there is indeed magic in medicine. In new techniques of surgery, American doctors lead the world. Every week there is news of another astonishing success. In 1900, Americans could expect to live to the age of 47.3 years. Now they can expect to live for 73.8 years.

Americans expect more and more from their doctors, but they have to pay more too. The cost of medical care is rising all the time, and new surgical techniques are the most expensive items of all. There are perhaps 75,000 people every year who need a new heart, but it would cost at least $7.5 billion to provide one for each of them.

Governments know that medicine is a vote-winner. If you want to get elected, you must pay the doctor's bills. Private insurance pays for 30 percent of medical costs in the U.S., and 40 percent of the money is paid by the government. But in spite of the $1 billion spent every day, the health of Americans is not as good as it could be. One in eight people have no medical insurance at all, and live in fear of becoming ill. As in other countries, drugs like heroin and cocaine have brought misery and sickness to thousands of young people. Medical care for poor people in city centers is not as good as the care given to their richer neighbors in the suburbs.

In spite of the problems, though, Americans, on the average, are getting healthier all the time. One reason is that they enjoy thinking and talking about their health. Some of the busiest clinics in the country never see a sick person. Their job is to check up on healthy people, to listen to their hearts, test their blood, and look for signs of any future illness.

"How am I doing, Doctor?" asks the worried businessman, as the doctor listens to his heart.

"Absolutely normal," says the doctor, and the businessman smiles in relief. He'll cheerfully pay this doctor's bill. The price is certainly not too high.

Chris Kuhlman— Midwife

If you walked into the Family Birthing Center in Concord, New Hampshire where Chris Kuhlman works, you might easily think you were in a private house. The furniture is soft and comfortable, the curtains bright and cheerful, and beautiful pictures of mothers and babies hang on the walls. It's completely different from the shiny modern hospitals where most American mothers give birth to their babies.

Chris Kuhlman, a midwife, is proud of it. "A family having a baby feels at home here," she says. "There's a room for the older children to play in, so that they can make a noise without disturbing the mother in her difficult work.

Modern medical technique— a scanner

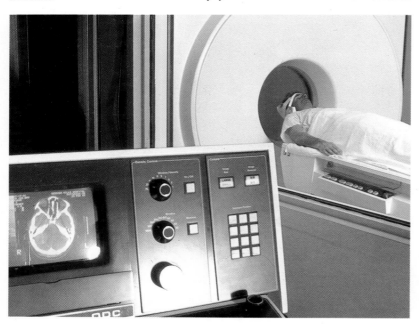

The mother herself has a nice bedroom, with an ordinary bed, and pretty lamps and curtains, like a home. Her husband stays with her, and he sometimes actually catches his own baby as it is born."

It costs about $1,000 to have a baby in an American hospital and only $614 in the birthing center. For this reason, poorer families often choose to use it. But it isn't only the price that mothers like. Many come because they don't like the doctors' ways of doing things, with their frightening machinery and powerful drugs.

"Having a baby is not an illness," says Chris. "Ninety-five percent of births are safe and easy, but doctors make women feel it's difficult and dangerous. Of course, if a mother needs hospital help, we don't accept her here. She has to go to a hospital."

Doctors do not always like Chris's ideas on childbirth. But she and her colleagues share at least one of the doctors' worst problems. She has to spend 50 percent of her income on insurance, in case a patient takes her to court.

Chris has already had a bad experience with lawyers. One of the babies she delivered was handicapped. The parents blamed her for it, and their lawyers tried to claim $4.8 million. The case made her life difficult for four long years, and although she won in the end, it was a painful experience.

There is another small sadness in Chris's life. She has no children of her own. But she laughs about it.

"I work an eighty-hour week," she says. "I wouldn't have time to be a mother myself." She points to the message printed on her apron. "The greatest joy in the world is to be a mother," it says, "and the second greatest joy is to be a midwife."

Chris Kuhlman at the Family Birthing Center in Concord, New Hampshire

Exercises

1 True or false?

1 The President is free to run the country as he likes.
2 Americans believe that businesspeople can run a business better than government officials.
3 Americans love their country even when they dislike its present government.
4 Wherever children go to school in America, they get exactly the same education.
5 At the times when most Americans are watching television, the programs are usually of an educational kind.
6 Medical care in the U.S. is very expensive.

2 Match the description with the institution.

1 The Senate
2 The Supreme Court
3 The Pentagon
4 West Point Academy
5 The "electronic church"
6 CBS

a) Headquarters of the Department of Defense
b) A TV network broadcasting to the entire country
c) A group of nine people who make important decisions about the way the country is run
d) Radio and TV stations owned by religious groups
e) One of the two houses of Congress
f) A training school for young army officers

3 Which of the following describe "hawks" and which describe "doves"? Which of them could describe either "hawks" or "doves"?

— they don't mind how much they spend on defense
— they are not sure if the armed forces really need everything they ask for
— they are afraid of spending too much on arms
— they wouldn't like America to appear weak
— they think America should always have more arms than the Soviet Union
— they think having too many arms may actually increase the chance of war

4 Discussion

Suppose that the following four programs were all on American television at the same time. Put them in the order of the size of audience you think would watch them:
1 = the program with the biggest audience, 4 = the one with the smallest audience. Compare your answer with other students' and discuss any differences.

"The Building of a New Submarine — report.

"Life on the American Railroads Today" — news story.

Christian service from Travis Road Baptist Church, with Dr. Gregory.

"A Child between Parents" — the story of a husband's battle with his wife to keep his child after the marriage has broken down.

Chapter Four

Americans at Work

Industry in Buffalo, New York State

To start with nothing, to work hard, and then to make a fortune—this is the American dream. People in the U.S.A. want more than anything else to be successful. And when they've made their money, they like to show it off by driving expensive cars and buying beautiful furniture for their homes.

One bad result of this is that people never seem to stop working. Some even hold two full-time jobs at the same time. This means that there is not much time for the good things in life, such as hours spent with one's family. Few families play games together, go for walks together, or even sit down every evening around the family table for a home-cooked meal.

The good result, though, is the confidence that many Americans have in themselves. They seem to feel that they can do anything, and get whatever they want if they try hard enough. It may take a lot of hard work to do well in America, but it's certainly exciting.

The Building Industry

Going Up and Up

In 1871, Mrs. O'Leary's cow kicked over a lantern and set fire to Chicago. Eighteen thousand buildings burned down, and three hundred people died. It was the end of the old Chicago, but it was also a new beginning. Out of the ashes grew a whole new style of building. The architects who rebuilt Chicago used steel to make strong frames that climbed so high they "scraped the sky." The skyscraper was invented.

The idea soon spread to other cities. Manhattan, in New York, became a forest of skyscrapers. All over the country, city skylines changed, as banks, big companies, and hotels pushed concrete, glass, and steel higher and higher. In "downtown" areas, where the stores and offices were found, earlier buildings disappeared to make way for the new style.

But while the downtown areas of many American cities become more modern, other parts are falling into ruin. In the inner-city areas, poorer people are crowded into old, badly cared-for buildings. There are too few jobs, and there is too much crime, and too little hope.

America's oldest cities, such as Boston, San Francisco, and New York, were built before the days of the automobile. Everyone had to live close to the city center. But the coming of the car changed all that. More and more of those who could afford to buy their own homes moved out to the new suburbs, where they could forget the noise, dirt, and crime of the city.

American suburban homes are extremely comfortable. Every house has a garage, there is usually a separate bedroom for each child in the family, two or even three bathrooms, and a large living room where guests can be entertained. It is not surprising that the value of these homes goes up and up.

For the 70 percent of Americans who own their own homes, the never-ending rise in house prices is a good thing. But for the others, housing is a serious problem. It is worst of all for the thousands of homeless people who sleep in the streets of every big city. But those who rent from landlords are not always much better off. As apartment buildings get older, many landlords are less willing to pay for the repairs. A Californian judge, Veronica Simmons, found a clever answer to that problem. She ordered a landlord to live in one of his own apartments for thirty days. Living with his own broken windows, cracked walls, and rats would be a better punishment, she decided, than sending him to prison.

Tom Sullivan— Ironworker

The men who build the great skyscrapers of New York City have a lot of respect for the weather. When the wind blows too hard, they stop work. When you're up on the hundredth floor, and there's nothing between you and the ground, it pays to be careful.

Tom Sullivan has been in the ironworking business for thirty years. He worked his way up to foreman, then to general foreman, and now he's a superintendent. He knows exactly how careful an ironworker has to be.

"We always build two floors at a time. So on

Skyscrapers in Chicago

the inside of the building, you can't fall more than two floors. On the outside, there's nothing but space. So if a man falls, he has to push himself inwards to land on the floor, not on the street down below."

Ironworkers earn good money these days, and their company has to provide for them if they get hurt. But you still have to have a special kind of courage to do the job.

"You can't look up at all. People don't realize that if you're standing on a beam, and you look up at the sky, you lose your balance very easily. It's not that bad to look down, except that it may be a little scary to some people. There's always the thought that comes into your mind, looking over the edge of the building, and wondering what it would be like to sort of jump off that building and fly. But I never tried it. Not yet, anyway!"

Tom has been so careful that he has had only small accidents. The worst happened on a bridge he was working on in New Rochelle. A piece of steel hit him on the chin, and he fell over eighteen feet. His wife prefers not to think about the dangers of the job. She's sensible. Her three sons are ironworkers too, and so were Tom's father and his two brothers. The Sullivan family, in fact, has played an important part in the building of New York City.

Tom is proud of his work. Sometimes, when

he has a day off, he walks around New York like a tourist. And everywhere he walks he sees a job he's worked on: a magnificent building like the Trump Tower, or the AT & T building, or one of the many bridges that join Manhattan Island to the other parts of New York.

"It just makes me feel good," says Tom. "When I look around, I can really say I have added a lot to New York City."

Above left:
The Trump Tower, Manhattan, New York
Above right:
Tom Sullivan in New York City

Banking and Finance

Wall Street

Wall Street is a place where the sun never shines. This doesn't mean that it has a different climate from the rest of New York City. It simply means that the buildings here in New York's financial center are so high that the street is always in the shade.

The people who work in the Wall Street area are too busy to worry about the weather. They are employed by great banking houses, such as J.P. Morgan, or giant financial companies like Merrill Lynch. They handle enormous sums of money every day. The savings of millions of Americans are in their hands.

Twenty years ago, life was a lot quieter on Wall Street. Many of the companies were old family firms. They had always been successful and did not see the need to work very hard for their money. Sons entering their fathers' businesses could come to work late, leave early, and be certain that no one would mind.

Those days are gone forever. Wall Street's big bosses still have magnificently furnished offices on the top floor, with wonderful views over New York harbor. But downstairs in the trading rooms, clever young people work feverishly at their computers sending money around the world.

Americans have never quite gotten used to trusting their banks. They remember too well the great Wall Street "crash" of 1929, when many banks closed and thousands of people lost their money. In order to keep the dangers small, American law prevents banks from becoming too big. No bank is supposed to have offices in more than one state. Perhaps this is why there are so many banks in America—nearly 15,000 of them.

The advantage of having so many small banks is that each one can get to know its customers, and can offer a personal service. The problem is that a traveler who has his or her money in a bank in Denver, Colorado, cannot easily get any money out from a bank in Memphis, Tennessee. But even this is changing now. Computers can send money so fast that the old system of American banks is breaking down.

Many Americans are not too happy about leaving their money in the bank. They want to see it grow, fast. That's one reason why many people spend as much money as they can on buying or improving houses. They know real estate prices often rise faster than anything else.

Grandpa might have put his money in a bag under the bed. But today, his grandson spends it on a new bedroom.

Ralph Di Fiore—The Best of Both Worlds

There are two sides to Ralph Di Fiore. One is the warm, friendly, home-loving family man. The other is the energetic, quick-thinking, ambitious New York City financier. Somehow, Ralph manages to get the best of both worlds.

Family man Ralph remembers his Italian childhood in Brooklyn, New York. Every Sunday, his grandmother cooked an enormous dinner for him, his parents, and his eighteen aunts, uncles, and cousins. He never forgot those happy days, even though college education and his first few jobs took him away from New York.

It was family man Ralph, who, on a skiing trip in Aspen, Colorado, went to rent a car, and fell in love with the girl in the car rentals office. Four months later, he and Claudia were married. And a few years after that, Ralph was very happy to come back home to New York.

Family man Ralph enjoys the beautiful home, with an acre of land and a swimming pool, that he has been able to provide for Claudia and their three children. He hates to catch the 6:10 train every morning to travel the forty miles from Darien, Connecticut, his wealthy suburb, into New York City. Every night, at 7:30, he is very pleased to get home so that he can play soccer with Jesse, his son.

But businessman Ralph loves to arrive at Grand Central Station every morning at 7:10 A.M., and get to work. He's the kind of person who needs to work hard, and to be successful. He spends sixty percent of his day telephoning people, persuading them to put their money into his firm, James Capel. That money will be invested all over the world, in Japan, Italy, Britain, northern Europe, Singapore, and Australia.

Ralph loves the excitement of the money markets, the politics, and the people. "The world markets change every day," he says. "There's always something going on. We all use computers now, but you still have to have trust and confidence in business. Even when you're dealing with billions of dollars, people don't have time to study every detail. They just have to trust you."

Businessman Ralph travels all the time.

Ralph Di Fiore on Wall Street

Even though he loves it, he can have too much of it. A few weeks ago he was in London, England. He went from the airport to a London office, sat down—and tried to fasten his seat belt. Perhaps businessman Ralph needs to take a break, and let family man Ralph have a little more time.

The Riches of the Earth

In 1848, Sam Brannan came running into San Francisco from Sutter's Fort in the Sierra. He had gold dust in his pockets, and the news spread fast. A few months later, the whole world knew about the hidden gold of California, and people rushed to the mountains to hunt for it. The "gold rush" had begun.

By the end of 1849, San Francisco was unrecognizable. In March 1848, the city had had only 1,000 citizens. By the summer of 1849, there were 5,000, and by 1850 the number had risen to 25,000. In the mining areas nearby, new towns grew with extraordinary speed. They were rough places for tough people, with names like "Hell's Delight" and "Swell-Head Diggings."

Few of the "forty-niners," as the gold rush miners were called, made much money. A few years later, the gold was all gone. The forty-niners became fishermen, storekeepers, or farmers. The old mining towns became "ghost towns," and today only the wind whistles down their empty streets.

California gold was to be only one of many exciting discoveries, for America has more natural wealth than almost any other country in the world. Some of it, like the huge amounts of silver in Nevada, was used up long ago. But there is still aluminum in Arkansas, copper in Arizona, and of course, the oilfields in places as far apart as Alaska in the north and Texas in the south.

"Black gold," as oil is sometimes called, has made more millionaires than yellow gold ever did. Money from oil paid for great cities like Houston in Texas, Tulsa in Oklahoma, and Denver in Colorado. In "Oil City U.S.A.," as Evenston, Wyoming was once called, oil workers could earn more than $1,000 a week.

But, like gold and silver before, oil riches do not last forever. When oil prices are high, Texans and Alaskans are rich. But when oil prices fall, they are the first to feel the difference. Those shining new office blocks in Houston and Dallas stand empty. Stores close down and many people are put out of work. Millionaires' helicopters no longer crowd the skies in the city centers, and Rolls-Royces and Mercedes appear in the used-car salesrooms.

Whatever happens to the oil prices, though, Americans need not worry yet. The country's natural wealth is so great that the U.S. will be able to keep the lights turned on for many years to come.

Paula Armstrong: A Career in Management

Paula Armstrong's office is high up in one of those beautiful steel and glass buildings that make up the city center of Dallas, Texas. From her window she can look down at the street far below, and out past the other skyscrapers to the endless flatness of Texas. It stretches for hundreds of miles in all directions, hiding its wealth below its dusty fields. Here and there, a piece of machinery sticks out of the ground, on top of which a metal arm nods up and down. It's a "nodding donkey," the top of an

Above:
Silverton, Colorado. Silver was found in the Rockies in the nineteenth century, and towns like Silverton grew up very quickly.
Right:
A "nodding donkey" oil well in Texas

oil well, pulling the wealth of Texas up above ground and into the hands of one of Dallas's many oil companies.

Paula is Hunt Oil's senior vice-president of information and human resources. Translated into plain English, that means she is in charge of her company's computers. She also runs the personnel department, and is in charge of the employees' welfare: their salaries, medical insurance, working conditions, etc.

Since Paula started her career, more and more women have taken top jobs in management. In the accounting firm where she first worked, nearly 60 percent of the management and professional staff are now women. Paula has come a long way, but she wants to go even further. She wants to manage her own company one day. She's lucky. Her husband, Frank, helps her as much as he can, and sometimes takes care of their nine-year-old daughter, Sarah, when Paula is at work.

Hunt Oil, where Paula now works, is an old family business. Mr. Ray Hunt is the chairman, and his mother and his three sisters own part of the company. Paula likes the family nature of the business.

"It's more friendly, more private than a big company," she says. "The family cares about their employees, and we get the chance to meet them."

"Dallas," a favorite TV soap opera, has given Americans the idea that Texan oilmen are tough and mean, and the women spend their time dressing up in expensive clothes. Paula laughs at that. "You don't see too many oilmen in Dallas with big hats and cowboy boots. And the businessmen here are not mean and dirty like you see them on TV. People in Dallas pull together and help each other."

Then she looks thoughtful. "Of course, there are rich women in town with nothing much to do. And up on the top floor of this building is the club where the big oilmen meet to do business. I should think a lot of interesting things go on up there..."

Paula Armstrong in her office in Dallas, Texas

The Automobile Industry

Where the Car is King

Ask an American man to choose between losing his house and losing his car, and he might easily choose to keep his car. A car, after all, gives you freedom, and freedom is what Americans want most of all.

The car is such an important part of American life that for many people it would be impossible to manage without it. A homemaker living in a suburb, for example, probably has a twenty-minute drive to take her children to school. She then turns the car around and drives for half an hour in another direction to get to her job in an office. To do her shopping, she has another long drive, so she plans carefully and buys food for two weeks in one trip.

The problem is, of course, that everyone else is driving to school or work at the same time. This results in serious traffic jams in all American cities at rush hour. In Los Angeles, which has almost no public transport, traffic can be a nightmare. There are 3.3 million workers traveling into Los Angeles from the suburbs every day, and 97 percent of them come by car. To keep the people moving, Los Angeles has built more and more roads, but even the 725 miles of freeways are not always enough. A small accident or breakdown at the busiest time of day can hold up the traffic for hours.

The American love affair with cars goes back to the earliest days of the automobile industry. One of the best-known names in American history is that of Henry Ford, who founded the great Ford Motor Company. He was the first to build cheap, popular cars that ordinary people could afford. His huge factories introduced modern methods of production and completely changed the face of American industry.

Today, only really poor families and those too old to drive do not own a motor vehicle. And their freedom is limited. But for the 87 percent who do have cars, there is hardly any need to use their legs. There are banks, fast-food restaurants, and movie theaters where you can withdraw money, eat a meal, or see a film without ever getting out of your car. There are even drive-in churches. It's surprising that some people remember how to walk at all.

Below:
Traffic on a freeway in Los Angeles
Bottom:
Car license plates from different states

Dick Edwards— A Self-Made Man

When Dick Edwards was a child, on a farm in Holdenville, Oklahoma, his father used horses instead of machines. Dick can remember picking cotton by hand, and helping with the peanut harvest.

But Dick has come a long, long way since then. He moved from farming into the oil industry, and then he started selling cars.

Now, Dick has his own car business, his own magnificent showroom, and sixty people working for him. They're busy all the time.

"Most people buy a new car every three years," says Dick. "And the kind of car they buy is changing. We sell more vans and pickups now than ordinary cars."

It's easy to see that Dick loves his work. "It's exciting," he says. "When people buy most things, they take a while to make up their minds, but when they buy a car, they see it—they want it. It's like falling in love with a pretty woman."

Dick fell in love a long time ago, and was married at the age of twenty-four. Janice, his wife, takes care of the home. "My wife has never worked," says Dick firmly, "and she's not going to work."

But Dick's three daughters all have jobs—in Dick's own business. Gayla, the oldest, is a clerk in the office, Tanice is the telephone operator, and Deana, the youngest, manages the car-rental part of the business. And they aren't the only members of the family. Dick's brother, son-in-law, and nephew all work for him too.

Dick gets to work at 8:30 in the morning and leaves between 8:00 and 9:00 at night. "I work hard and long," he says, "and my managers work hard and long. If they don't like to work, they can get themselves another job."

But Dick believes in relaxing too. He likes to hunt, and takes his gun out sometimes to shoot wild birds. He also loves horseback riding, and he and Janice keep their own horses. This year they're going off to Missouri on a ten-day trail ride. The horses will travel in the trailer, and the Edwards will go in their motor home.

Things certainly have changed since Dick was a boy. In those days, the horses pulled the machines. Now, it's the machines that carry the horses.

Dick Edwards outside his automobile showroom

On the Move

Americans love speed. They like to cook in microwave ovens, they prefer making phone calls to writing letters, and they like to travel by air rather than bus or train. And when they send a package, they want it to arrive tomorrow, not next week.

In a country the size of the U.S., that's not easy. Distances are enormous, and with the speed limit on most highways at only 55 mph, it takes a long time for things to go by land. Everything that can fly, does.

Offering a quick service is a sure way to make money in the States. Fast-delivery companies are getting more business all the time. One of the biggest of them, Federal Express, will deliver a computer disk in just a few hours to a forgetful businessman who left his bag behind. Or it will get a tuxedo to a college student away from home who has an unexpected date and nothing to wear. And if anyone wants to say "I'm sorry," or "I love you," or "Happy birthday," Roseland Express will send a dozen fresh roses anywhere in the U.S.A. within twelve hours.

Not everyone in the States likes speed, though. Some people, in fact, refuse to be hurried. The Amish people in Pennsylvania and the Midwest stopped the clock in the eighteenth century. They still live in the unhurried style of those days, refusing to use cars, telephones, televisions, or any other modern invention. In their historical clothes and horse-drawn carriages, they are living reminders of the slower life of earlier times.

Few Americans live in such peace as the Amish people enjoy. In fact, Americans are always on the move. Nearly half the population moves at least once every five years, and some more often than that. Most people move to a suburb or town nearby, but many pack all their furniture and belongings into a van and move to the other side of America. A girl who has grown up in Chicago might study in New York, and find her first job in Philadelphia. She might move to California to look for better work, marry a man from Des Moines, and move back to be near his family in Iowa. At last, when her children have grown up, she might get tired of the cold winters, and retire to Florida to spend her old age sitting in the sun.

So, if you want to write a letter to a friend who lives in Missouri, do it now. By this time next year, she might have moved to Maryland, or Michigan, or Minnesota.

Chuck Joyner— Interstate Trucker

Chuck was in Texas last Friday. He delivered part of his load in Houston, then went up to Oklahoma City where he delivered some more. On Monday night he picked up another load in Tulsa, Oklahoma, and by Tuesday he was in Albuquerque, New Mexico. On Wednesday he stopped in Arizona on his way to Burbank, California. He has gone 3,500 miles in a week, and he has been on the road

for eight and a half weeks since he set off from Seattle, Washington.

Chuck is proud of his truck. It's the first he has owned. That's why he had the words "First Born" painted on the side. In a few weeks, he will have paid back all the money he borrowed in order to buy it.

He's right to be proud of his "First Born." It doesn't only look good on the outside, it's comfortable inside too. Behind the driver's seat is the bed where Chuck sleeps when he's on the road. He carries his own food, too, in a tiny refrigerator. He even has a freezer and a TV set. It's very different from the kind of truck Chuck's father drove, in the bad old days, when truckers had to drive very long hours, and there was no air-conditioning.

Chuck enjoys being a trucker, but his first love was motorcycles. He used to be a champion motorcycle racer, and he won over a thousand trophies in his many years on the racetracks. His greatest moment was at Peoria, Illinois, in 1978, when he won the TT National Championship. But he paid a heavy price for his success.

"I broke a lot, nearly every bone in my body except my legs. Which is a little strange when you think about it. Most people break their legs first. But I didn't give up. There are ninety-nine national motorcycling racing numbers in the world, and I was number sixty."

Chuck doesn't break his bones anymore. He has problems with blown-out tires instead. It costs $300 to put a new tire on First Born. He had to put one on thirty miles back, and now another needs changing. But it's still worth it.

"The best thing is the freedom," he says. "I do what I want to do. I work for myself."

When Chuck has paid off the money for his truck, he's looking forward to doing something for his parents. "My folks are retired, and I want to help them," he says. "After raising a whole family, I want them to go play for a while."

Chuck Joyner with "First Born"

Changing Industries

From Cars to Computers

A young man (or, very seldom, a young woman) with no money and little education decides he must get to the top. He works all day, studies at night, and looks around for a chance to get rich. He discovers that all his friends like eating his mother's home-made pizzas. He learns how to make them and starts selling them at school. He leaves his job and opens a pizza restaurant. It is a great success, so he opens another, then another. Five years later, he has made his first million dollars. He is the perfect example of the successful American businessman.

Stories like this are very popular in the States. Rich men who started out with nothing and built up huge fortunes are national heroes. Every schoolchild has heard of Henry Ford, John D. Rockefeller, and Andrew Carnegie. People like to believe that the chance to get rich is there for anyone, however poor, who is brave, smart, and hardworking enough to take it.

The American admiration for business success is as strong as ever. Modern heroes are men like Steven Jobs, who founded the Apple computer business, and Lee Iacocca of Chrysler, whose book describing his road to success was a bestseller. But in spite of these stories, many people are worried about their country's industry. They see factories closing and people losing their jobs. They point to towns like Homestead, Pennsylvania, where 14,000 people once worked in a giant steel factory. Now the factory is closed and over half the town is unemployed.

"The trouble is," older people say, "that young people don't work as hard as they used to." In fact, Americans work very hard. Most people have only two or three weeks' vacation a year, and work for at least forty hours a week. The trouble is that American industry itself is changing. Old industries, like steel, textiles, and shoes, cannot keep their prices low enough. New industries, that use computer techniques, do not need to employ many people. As a result, people who worked in the factories of ten years ago are working in restaurants, offices, or airlines today.

Americans are usually optimistic about the future. They like to think that they need only keep going when times are hard. An old World War II poster expressed it well. "The difficult we do immediately," it said. "The impossible takes a little longer."

A steelworks in Pittsburgh, Pennsylvania

Doreen Fairbairn—
The "Brain Drain"

When Doreen Fairbairn got her first job at an engineering company in England, she was told, "You'll never earn a proper salary because you're a woman." Doreen had a good degree in physics, but she wasn't surprised. It seemed normal in those days that good jobs in industry were closed to women.

But that manager couldn't have been more wrong. At fifty-four, Doreen is earning a very good salary, and she's still moving up in her career.

The key to Doreen's success is that she has never stopped learning. She went back to school almost as soon as she graduated, because she wanted to work in the new transistor industry. After several different jobs, she moved to an American firm called Texas Instruments. A long time before, between classes at college, she had found time to fall in love, and now, years later, when her fiancé had finished his Ph.D. in chemistry, Doreen was married.

At that time, a lot of American companies were looking for clever young scientists from abroad. They could usually offer better working conditions and more money than British or other European firms. The stream of brilliant scientists going to America became a flood. It was called "the brain drain." In 1962, Doreen and her husband joined it, and moved across the Atlantic to Boston.

Since then, Doreen and her husband have watched Boston develop into one of the most exciting areas for "hi-tech" industry in the U.S. They have been exciting years for Doreen too. Since 1972, she has worked at Polaroid, where she is now a principal engineer. She is in charge of five other engineers, and it is her job to look after and repair the test equipment that Polaroid uses to build their cameras. Polaroid has sent her all over the United States, to Germany and Holland in Europe, and even to Hong Kong and Japan.

"I really enjoy my travels," says Doreen. "People don't expect an engineer to be a woman. They don't know how to treat me. Anyway, they certainly remember the day Mrs. Fairbairn came to visit!"

Doreen still hasn't stopped learning. She has just finished another course of study, and now has her Master of Business Administration degree. But when she's not working, she knows how to enjoy herself. In her free time, she sings in a choir that performs classical music. Her eyes light up when she talks about it. "Put me with ten or twenty other sopranos," she laughs, "and I have a lot of fun."

Doreen Fairbairn at Polaroid, Boston, Massachusetts

Big Business

Delicious and Refreshing?

On May 8, 1886, Dr. John Styth Pemberton, a chemist, carried a bottle down the street in Atlanta, Georgia, to Jacob's Pharmacy on the corner. There, soda water was added to it, and the new drink was put on sale for five cents a bottle. The drink contained sugar, water, the leaves of the coca plant, and the juice of the kola nut. Dr. Pemberton's partner, Frank Robinson, thought of a name for it.

"Coca-Cola," he said. "The two Cs would look well in advertising."

For the first year of its life, Coca-Cola sold only thirteen drinks a day. By its hundredth birthday, in 1986, it was selling 7.9 billion dollars' worth a year. Not much of the money went into John Pemberton's pocket. He died two years after he had invented Coca-Cola, and Asa G. Candler, a clever businessman, bought the business for $2,300.

From then on, Coca-Cola's success was all due to advertising. The words *Coca-Cola, delicious and refreshing*, in flowing, graceful writing, were soon to be seen everywhere: on calendars, clocks, trays, and walls. The more people heard of it, the more people wanted it, and by 1895, Candler could say, "Coca-Cola is now sold and drunk in every state in the United States."

But the great days of Coca-Cola were still to come. In World War II, the company made a promise that every American soldier, sailor, and airman could have a Coke for five cents a bottle, anywhere in the world. The company knew they would lose money, but it was worth it. In one smart move they made sure that five billion bottles of Coke would find their way around the world, creating new demand in more countries. They also knew that the idea of Coca-Cola as something truly, especially American would be strengthened.

In the years that followed the war, Coca-Cola managed to make itself one of the most powerful symbols of America both inside and outside the States. "Drink Coca-Cola, and you will share in the American dream," the advertisements seem to say.

So what is in this magic drink that has become the most successful product in world history? That secret is locked up in a bank in Atlanta, and only a few people alive know the exact recipe.

One very important question remains: Is Coca-Cola good for you? Dentists say that sugary drinks like Coca-Cola harm your teeth. Doctors say they add to problems of fatness that lead to heart disease. Delicious and refreshing? Maybe.

José Montoya— Longing to Travel

Today, in Santa Fe, they're making Dr. Pepper, Canada Dry, Coca-Cola, Diet Coke, and Cherry Coke in ten-ounce glass bottles. Yesterday, they were filling the big, two-liter bottles. José Montoya has brought in today's bottles to get

A World War II Coca-Cola advertisement

the line started. Now he's watching to make sure it doesn't stop. If it does break down, he'll have to repair it.

Working at Coca-Cola keeps José busy all day long, but he doesn't mind. He has done all kinds of work, out on the farm, or in factories like this one. This job suits him fine.

José has a lot of time for dreaming—and remembering. He left home when he was fifteen, and for two years he traveled around in Wyoming, Colorado, Texas, and New Mexico. He took any work he could find, and he had so little money that sometimes he had to sleep by the side of the road.

"I had a lot of adventures," says José, smiling. "Well, I was young."

At seventeen, José decided it was time to settle down. He got married, and his first daughter, Gloria, was born a year later. Shirley, his youngest, followed after a gap of twelve years. The girls are grown up now, and José is beginning to feel restless again.

"Sometimes I guess I'll stay here," he says, "but you never can tell. If I have to leave for some reason, I'd like to travel. Just work in one place for a few months and then go on. But Rose, my wife, she hates the idea of change. She doesn't like to go where she doesn't know the people. I wanted my daughters to join the army. I never did it, because I hurt my back, and I wanted them to do it. That way they could have traveled. But I guess they didn't want to." His face brightens again.

"Well, anyway, we went to Las Vegas last year, in Nevada. I lost a little money. I didn't care. It's a twenty-four hour town—never in the dark."

José doesn't travel as much as he'd like to, but he keeps himself busy. In his spare time he buys dolls, makes lovely, big dresses for them, then turns them into stands for lamps. He does all the electrical work and sells them. One day, perhaps, he'll have enough money to pay for his best dream of all.

"You know where I'd really like to go? To Africa, to the jungles. I've seen it on TV, and I'd like to go there one day and help those people over there."

José Montoya bottling Coca-Cola

Exercises

1 Match the description with the city.

1 Chicago	a)	Where 50 percent of the working population are without a job.
2 New York	b)	Contains the offices of many large oil companies.
3 San Francisco	c)	Where Coca-Cola was "born."
4 Houston, Texas	d)	One of the world's main financial centers.
5 Los Angeles	e)	Where the first skyscrapers were built following a terrible fire.
6 Homestead, Pennsylvania	f)	Its population increased in only two years from 1,000 to 25,000.
7 Atlanta, Georgia	g)	Where there are almost no buses or trains.

2 True or false?

1 In large American cities there are very great differences between the living conditions of rich and poor.

2 A Californian judge made a landlord live in one of his own apartments because she thought it would teach him to be fairer to his tenants.

3 Only a few Americans can afford to buy a home of their own.

4 In 1871 the Chicago authorities burned down the older buildings of their city, so that skyscrapers could be built.

5 Many Americans believe they can make money quickest by buying and selling houses.

6 Most Americans prefer to spend their money on their home, rather than putting it in a bank.

7 It was the discovery of gold which suddenly turned San Francisco into a city.

8 Most Americans feel they can't lead an active life without a car of their own.

9 The "brain drain" means well-qualified professional people move from a country where salaries and working conditions are poor, to another country where salaries and conditions are better.

10 The Coca-Cola company improved their business during World War II.

3 Find these figures from the text and write them in the boxes.
Then say whether you think each figure is high or low. Give reasons for your opinions.

Percentage of people in the U.S. who have their own car	
Percentage of people who come to work by car in Los Angeles	
Number of banks in the U.S.	
Percentage of Americans who own their own homes	
Speed limit on most highways	

4 Answer these questions.

1 How many examples can you give of the Americans' love of speed?

2 How many examples can you give of their love of freedom?

3 Are the Amish people typical Americans? Why (not)?

4 What do you understand by "the American love affair with cars"?

5 Discussion

1 Why do Americans work so hard? Do they feel the same way about work as people in your country?

2 Look back at the people in this chapter. Which do you think is the best example of someone who has made the American dream come true, and why? Do you think any of them has entirely failed in his/her attempt to make the dream come true?

Chapter Five

Americans at Play

Surfing in Hawaii

Y ou might expect people who work so hard to really relax when their work is done. But Americans take even their free time seriously. Almost everything they do, even on vacation, seems to have a goal. If they exercise, it is because they want to be healthier, or to get fit. If they go to a concert or to the theater, it is because they feel that culture and the arts are good for their minds. If they play a ballgame, it is because they want to win. "I used to think that winning was important. Now I think it's everything," said one well-known athlete.

Maybe this is the reason why Americans watch so much television. No one could say that most of the popular programs have a serious goal. Perhaps it's a good thing. After all, everyone needs to relax sometime.

Sport

Ballgames

Have you heard of the Detroit Tigers, or the Kansas City Royals, or the Cincinnati Reds? No, they're not names of bus companies, or even of student clubs. They are some of America's best-known baseball teams.

In the rest of the world, the most exciting sports events are the internationals, but in the States these are infrequent. This is because few other countries play baseball, basketball, and American football, the favorite American games. So instead of playing against other countries, the big cities of America play against each other. In the summer, baseball news is always on TV. And in the winter, it's the football season, with the players dressed like spacemen and a show-business atmosphere.

Show business, in fact, is a good description of big American matches. The teams are owned by wealthy businessmen, who run them with the same business sense as they run their own companies. They hire marching bands, and teams of attractive young women in fantastic costumes to lead the cheering. The team organizers will do anything to make sure their teams appear on TV. "I'll play at midnight, if that's what TV wants," Bear Bryant, coach of the University of Alabama's football team once said.

Billy Veeck, who owned the St. Louis Browns baseball team, was well known for his ideas. To bring the crowds in, he even had an exploding scoreboard made. "If you want to give away 50,000 beers," he once said, "give them all to one fan." That, he thought, would really get into the news.

You have to be young, male, and very strong to play for one of the professional baseball or football teams. But those are not the only ballgames in the U.S. Basketball is played in every high school and college, by both boys and girls. But once students have left school, few continue to play. For most Americans, television is the nearest they'll ever get to a real ballgame.

For a country that sells so much abroad, America has been slow to sell its ballgames. But there are signs that this is changing. Baseball has been played seriously for a long time in Japan, the West Indies, and Central America. Now, American football is following, even to Europe.

So if you haven't heard of the Chicago Bears, the Pittsburgh Steelers, or the New York Jets, don't worry. You'll soon be watching the London Ravens, the Frankfurt Lions, and the Keio University Unicorns.

Below left:
Basketball — the Los Angeles Lakers play the Denver Nuggets
Below right:
Football — the Chicago Bears play the San Francisco 49ers ("Sweetness" is on the right)

Walter Payton—
A Bear Called "Sweetness"

The people of Chicago have learned to be tough. Their history of gangsters is well known. And the Chicago Bears, their football team, are tough like their town. There isn't anyone who can show them anything new about the game.

The Chicago Bears are great because their players are great. Every American has heard of Jim McMahon, the one with the dark glasses and the strange haircut. McMahon is also the one who doesn't like being told what to do. When Bears' coach Mike Ditka told him to wear a tie, McMahon did—but without a shirt. Almost as famous is Willie Gault. He's the one who surprised everyone by going on stage with the Chicago City Ballet, after only five lessons, and giving a great performance. Then there's William "the Refrigerator" Perry. He's the one who eats six chickens and several steaks for dinner, and who beats the other side by simply squashing them flat.

But everyone agrees that the greatest of all is the Bears' running back, Walter Payton, who is perhaps the best all-round player there has ever been. He's quieter than the others. You won't see him wearing flashy clothes, like Jim McMahon, or advertising Coca-Cola on TV like the Refrigerator. He's smaller than the others too, but his legs and arms are like steel. He's the one they call "Sweetness."

Sweetness has won almost every prize and broken every record in American football. He has been the All-American Black Athlete of the Year. The newspapers have to hunt for words to describe his game. "The greatest football player in history," "a running, jumping, catching superman," "a magician," they call him. Not surprisingly. Walter Payton is the best paid of the Chicago Bears. Is he worth over a million dollars a year? He smiles when you ask him that question. "The way I feel, they couldn't even pay me what I'm worth," he says.

What makes Sweetness so good? "I guess it's mental control," he says. "The way you think is the way you are. I always try to do better than last year. There's always one more yard, one more block, one less mistake."

Mardi Gras in New Orleans

Party Time

You will not be surprised to hear that every true American waves a flag on July 4th. This is the day when Americans remember the beginnings of their nation. And you would expect every true American to sit at the family table and eat turkey on Thanksgiving Day in November. This is when they thank God for the good things in their lives, and remember the courage of the first Europeans who landed in America.

You might, on the other hand, be surprised to hear how many Americans go out to follow the dancing lion on the Chinese New Year. Or how many meet with their families at Passover, the Jewish festival. Or how many listen to bagpipe music and drink whisky on Burns Night, a traditional Scottish festival.

There are special festivals in different parts of the States. They show how many different nations came together to make the American nation. In New Orleans, for example, there's the old French festival of Mardi Gras. March in Miami, Florida, is carnival time when the thousands of Spanish speakers take to the streets in wonderful costumes. In Chicago, on St. Patrick's Day (the national day of the Irish)

Irish green is everywhere. People wear green clothes, drink green beer, and even the Chicago River is colored green for the day. In New York, there will be special food and special parties for Irish, Italian, Puerto Rican, Jewish, and Chinese days. In the Midwest, people remember the European festivals.

The truth is that Americans love parties. But perhaps the best parties of all are private, family ones. Some, like Halloween, are especially for the children. At the end of October, they dress up as ghosts or witches and go from house to house asking for candy or cookies. Another very American kind of party is a "shower." A group of friends get together to give presents to someone who is getting married or having a baby.

Whatever the reason, Americans love to invite people to their homes, and they work hard to make their homes look good and their food taste delicious. Is it little Susan's birthday? Her friends come in for the party and have cake and ice cream. The Fourth of July? A group of friends go out together for a picnic. And what about Presidents' Day in February? There will be cherry pie at home for everyone, of course.

The Lake Family at Thanksgiving

The turkey is already on the table. The potatoes and other vegetables are waiting to be served. Anne Lake has just hurried in from the kitchen and sat down at the table. The children are hungry, but they're being careful. They're wearing their best clothes today, and they don't want to get them dirty.

Ralph stands up. Everyone shuts their eyes.

"Dear Lord," he prays, "together, on this Thanksgiving Day, we thank you for the many blessings we have received during this past year. Amen."

"Amen," say Anne and the children. And now the dinner can begin.

Usually, Americans have a big family party at the Thanksgiving dinner, with grandparents,

aunts, and uncles. Schools and offices are closed, and the airports are busy with millions of people going to see their families. But this year, the Lakes are on their own.

The first Thanksgiving was celebrated in 1621 by the "Pilgrim Fathers," some of the first Europeans who came to live in North America. At the end of the first year in their new land, they made a feast. They cooked the turkeys, pumpkins, and corn which the Indians had taught them to eat, and invited the Indians to share the meal. They said prayers, and thanked God that they were still alive.

Anne and Ralph have exciting family stories to tell about the time long ago, when Thanksgiving had a very real meaning for everyone. Anne's family arrived in 1640, soon after the first Thanksgiving. They nearly played an important part in American history. George

Washington wanted to marry one of Anne's great-great-grandmothers. The girl's father did not like George, so she had to refuse him. Thomas Jefferson wanted to marry another of Anne's ancestors, but she refused to marry him.

Ralph also has interesting stories to tell. In the 1820s, his ancestors sailed down the Ohio River to Kentucky. It was a dangerous journey. Indians hid on rocks along the river, and shot at the people in the boats below.

Today, history is pretty much forgotten. The Lakes are too busy celebrating. After dinner, like most other Americans, they'll watch the big football game on TV. But first, it's time for dessert. Everyone knows what it will be. The children even sing a song about it.

"Hurrah for the fun! Is the pudding done? Hurrah for the pumpkin pie!"

Thanksgiving dinner at the Lakes. The dolls on the table represent the Pilgrim Fathers and the Indians who helped them

Fashion and Beauty

A Billion-Dollar Business

Beauty, said our grandmothers, is only skin-deep. This is no doubt true, but Americans have discovered that there is a lot you can do to your skin. The strange thing is that white people want their skins to look browner, while black people want their skins to look whiter. Old people want to look younger, teenagers want to look older, and nearly everyone wants to look thinner.

Americans spend billions of dollars a year on the beauty industry. About $300 million is spent in "tanning salons" where people go to get brown. They may not be able to afford a holiday in a warmer climate, but they can afford ten dollars for half an hour on a sun bed under an electric sun.

Doctors and dentists can also join the beauty business. Dentists have done their work so well that American teeth are now 50 percent healthier than they were in 1970. To keep themselves in a job, many dentists now work on "smile repair," whitening, straightening, and beautifying wherever they can. And while dentists work on the perfect smile, specialist doctors remove fat, shorten noses, and tighten loose skin on old faces.

Beauty was once a matter for women, but now men are joining in. They buy one billion dollars' worth of creams, after-shave preparations, and even makeup every year.

To look really good, of course, you must wear the right clothes. Until the 1970s, Paris was the fashion capital of the world and most American designers usually did no more than copy European ideas. Most Americans chose safe, familiar clothes, and millions bought everything, including shoes and underwear, from a mail-order catalog. Twelve million American families still order at least some of their clothes from the Sears catalog, which has been America's biggest seller for nearly a hundred years.

Now, even Sears is getting a new fashionable look because American fashion design is growing more confident and exciting all the time. Internationally famous designers include Norma Kamali, Ralph Lauren, and Calvin Klein, whose daring advertisements have changed the way men think about underwear. The Seventh Avenue area of New York City, the center of American fashion, is alive with new, young ideas.

Beauty may be only skin-deep, but there's a lot of it to see in America. If you don't believe me, go and see a beauty contest. When the girls put on their bathing suits, you'll see not only beauty, but plenty of skin as well.

Michelle Royer—Miss Texas

You won't find this easy to believe, but Michelle Royer was a shy little girl, who didn't take much interest in makeup and clothes. She used to watch the beauty pageants on TV and she never imagined that she would one day be crowned a beauty queen herself.

"I wasn't a cheerleader," she says. "I wasn't very popular. But there was always this eager young woman inside, trying to come out."

One Christmas vacation, Michelle suddenly decided to try for a beauty contest. To her surprise, she received second prize. To her surprise also, she found she liked the feeling of being up on the stage. She went on, winning some contests, doing less well in others, and learning all the time, about how to move, how to dress, how to talk. And when at last she was crowned Miss Texas over 109 other young women, she had her reward for all her hard work.

"I was shocked when they called my name," she says. "But now, after two months, I'm really beginning to enjoy myself."

Texans are serious about their beauty queen. They shower her with prizes. Michelle won a car, a full-length fur coat, $18,000 in cash, and an apartment for a year, as well as clothes, shoes, jewelry, purses, and dozens of smaller gifts.

They also make Miss Texas work. "I belong to Texas this year," says Michelle. "My car has 'Miss Texas' written on it, and when people see it they shout 'Hey! It's Miss Texas!' And the children smile and wave at me. So I spend time making myself look as good as possible for them. It takes me about two hours to get dressed. And I travel about to festivals, or parades, or high schools. And I work for the people who've given me gifts, and do advertising for them."

Michelle doesn't want to stop at Miss Texas. There's the Miss U.S.A. contest next year, and Miss Universe after that. She's preparing her clothes already. She's also preparing her mind. She imagines herself on the stage, winning the prize. She watches movies about people who don't expect to do well, and who come out first in the end. She plans her answers to the questions she'll be asked.

It doesn't matter how pretty you are, you can't be a beauty queen forever. When it's time to put the crowns away, Michelle would like to be a model. After that, she wants to go back to school and become a doctor so that she can help sick children. There's also the question of a husband.

"I haven't found Mr. Right yet," she says, "but I know he's out there somewhere, and I'm always looking for him."

Michelle Royer, who went on to win the Miss U.S.A. contest

Show Business

That Old Silver Screen

Where in the world can you take an hour's train ride, and pass a forest, a London street, a scene from the Wild West, and a burning building that never burns down? There's only one place, and that's Hollywood, in California. The scenes you see from the tourist train are film sets in Universal Studios, one of the oldest and largest movie companies in America.

A visit to Universal brings back memories of the great days of Hollywood, the multi-million-dollar films and the exciting, glamorous stars. But they are mostly memories. Hollywood isn't quite the same as it used to be. Costs have gone up and confidence has gone down. Moviemakers are afraid to spend their money on expensive new ideas. Instead, they repeat old ones over and over.

The film industry is changing fast. Teenagers still go out to the movies. The theater is a good place to meet friends away from home. But older people mostly stay home to watch films made for TV, or long-running series, on their own televisions or video players. Big TV series, like "Dynasty," have become as impor-tant to Hollywood as expensive movies. These "soap operas," as they are called, show rich, powerful families living in beautiful homes and wearing glamorous clothes. But the actors and actresses are nearly all middle-aged, like many of the people who watch them.

Although it is soap operas that are keeping the filmmakers of Hollywood in business, big films are still being made in America. But more and more of them are made outside Hollywood. New York is the most important new center, but there are many others as well. Moviemakers have discovered that they don't need Hollywood anymore. Modern cameras and equipment are smaller and lighter. They can be taken to film real streets and real houses instead of expensively made copies in a studio. Other states, especially Florida and Texas, are working hard to take the film business away from California. They are offering better working conditions, lower costs, and less official paperwork.

But Hollywood is fighting back. The state of California is trying hard to keep its best-known industry. The silver screen of Hollywood is, after all, one of the great traditions of America. "The silver screen of Miami" doesn't sound quite the same.

A film set at Universal Studios in Hollywood

Monique Cintron—
Fame on Broadway

Monique Cintron

Monique was the sort of child who couldn't sit still. She was always jumping around. Now, at the age of twenty-one, she's still doing it, but she's being paid for it. Acting, singing, and dancing are her career.

Monique gave her first real performance when she was only eight years old. Her mother, also an actress, was working with a street-theater company. They needed a child for the play, and Monique got the part.

"It was a wonderful experience," she says. "The adults showed me how to move, and when, and where."

Monique wanted to go on dancing, but there was no money to pay for classes. Her parents had divorced when she was only three, and her mother had two other children to look after. But Monique was still determined to get into the New York High School of Performing Arts, which trains young people with special talents.

"The other kids had done ballet for years," she remembers. "Some of the little girls were real prima ballerinas. I had only had one month of lessons, from a teacher who let us pay half price. But my mother said, 'Just tell them the truth. They'll see if you're a dancer or not. Go in there and dance.' So I did, and I got in." She stops talking for a moment.

"My mom has always been there for me. She really believes in me."

After high school came college, and endless jobs to earn money. Monique even delivered bouquets of balloons for a greetings-card company. It was while she was at college that her lucky chance came. She met a girlfriend on the subway one day.

"I'm going to an audition," the friend said. "Why don't you come?"

The audition was for a film called *Fast Forward*, directed by Sidney Poitier. Three thousand people were interviewed, and seven were accepted. Monique was one of them. At eighteen, she found herself in Hollywood, among all the fun, the sun, the sand, and the expensive cars. Suddenly she had money. She was independent.

Now Monique's greatest wish is about to come true. She has been offered a part in the Broadway show *Madam Rosa*, directed by Harold Prince, America's best-known musical director. She was very nervous at the audition.

"I crossed my fingers, and I just sang, and danced, and read," she says. It worked. She got the part. Her smile grows bigger than ever. "All my life, I just wanted Broadway, Broadway, Broadway, and now it's really going to happen."

Music

A jazz club in New Orleans

From Big to Small

Americans buy four billion dollars' worth of records every year. That is a whole lot of music. But those four billion dollars are not all spent on one kind of music. Jazz, country and western, rock, and pop each have their own musicians, clubs, and followers.

Traditionally, New Orleans in the south was the city of jazz. Nashville, Tennessee, was the home of country and western, and rock music, of course, is wherever the big rock stars take it. But all that is changing now. The best jazz is to be found in New York or Los Angeles. Country and western music is played in clubs and bars in every city in the U.S. And rock music, which once belonged to huge concerts in enormous stadiums, is heard in every small place where people want to dance.

From big to small. That is one change in today's music world. Of course, there are still stars like Michael Jackson or Madonna, who rise suddenly to the top and may fall again just as suddenly. For a time, they are followed by crowds of adoring "Wanna be's" ("We wanna [*want to*] be like Madonna!"). But many Americans are rediscovering the pleasure of listening to music nearer to home. They don't want to drive long distances to a crowded concert hall. They would rather dance to the music of a local band in a small club near home.

There's another important change in the air. The king of rock, Elvis Presley, used to sing about love. Today's biggest rock star, the "Boss," Bruce Springsteen, worries about the poor and the hungry. His songs are political, and they don't try to hide it. And Springsteen is not the only one. Top rock musicians have joined together to make money for the hungry in Africa. They have made money for poor farmers in the U.S., and there is more "music aid" to come.

Things change so fast in the world of popular music that anything you say today will no longer be true tomorrow. But one thing will certainly remain. The record companies will continue to sell their billions of dollars' worth of records every year.

Joe Ely—
A hundred miles to go

"A hundred miles I've got to go tomorrow," sings Joe Ely, "and leave you here with your sorrow." It isn't just a song for him. Tomorrow he'll be traveling more than a hundred miles, and he'll be going even further the day after. Traveling and singing, singing and traveling—that's Joe Ely's life.

"I got my education from the road," he says. "I went to Europe with a theater company when I was eighteen. We moved around all the time from one country to another. I earned sixty dollars a week, and slept where I was, even in the theater sometimes."

It was then that Joe started writing music and songs. His rhythm is rock 'n' roll, but the words are more in the country style. It's a great combination.

Joe is well known now, in the U.S. and in Europe, but he still learns from his travels. He writes his best songs when he's on the move.

"Sometimes a song just comes running into your head from somewhere," he says. "I've written songs on tables in restaurants, on menu cards, even on the wall. That's what I love—to take an idea, and make a song of it, and play it. After you play it, where does it go? It's like moving air. It blows out of the window, through the cracks in the door. But it stays in your mind. If someone hears a song of mine, and takes it away with them, that's cool. That's great."

Between his travels, Joe is at home in Austin, Texas, with his wife, Sharon, and their small daughter, Marie Elena. But when he's on the road, life goes crazy again. He and his band sleep in a different place every night, and eat any time, anywhere.

Some singers take drugs to keep themselves going. "I've used drugs," says Joe. "I thought they would be a key to unlock doors in my head. But drugs are like locks, not keys. They open a few doors, but they shut many others."

The best times for Joe are when he's on stage, playing, and everything goes just right.

"Sometimes I don't even have to think about what I'm doing," he says. "The music comes right through me. Everyone in the band feels the same, like the music's playing itself. It doesn't matter then if you're in Antarctica or Katmandu. You just have to let it go."

Joe Ely on the road

Food

Fifty Billion Hamburgers

What *is* American food? Hamburgers and hot dogs? Fried chicken and giant steaks? Well, yes. But spaghetti and pizza are American too, and so is sweet and sour pork. The fact is that Americans eat every kind of food imaginable. There are, for example, more than 1,000 Chinese restaurants in New York City alone.

At the same time, people in the States still like to think of some kinds of food as especially American. They like the idea of the American family sitting around the table eating turkey at Thanksgiving. They like to think of "Mom" as the best cook in the world, even if their own mother never did much cooking. "As American as apple pie," and "Like Mother makes it" are popular expressions.

The truth is, though, that families in the U.S.

eat together less often than they used to. Instead of meeting at the dinner table, families often meet in the kitchen, around the refrigerator. There's no time for old-fashioned cooking. Quick snacks all through the day have taken its place. And to save trouble, people eat wherever they like, in the street, in front of the TV, or at their desks.

An enormous fast-food industry gives hungry Americans the snacks they want when they want them. Ice cream, popcorn, and hot dogs are on sale everywhere. Best known, perhaps, is the McDonald's hamburger business. With an American love for numbers, McDonald's count the hamburgers they sell. Hamburger number one was sold in 1948. Hamburger number fifty billion was eaten in November 1984.

But if more and more Americans eat fast food, more and more Americans also worry about it. Fast food makes you fat, and Americans are the fattest people in the world. They are also the most interested in their health, and snack food is not healthy. The fashion for health food is growing all the time. Among middle-class people, salads, beans, and fruit have taken the place of steak and ice cream. Drinking is going down too. Only 67 percent of adults drink alcohol at all, and one-third of those drink less than they used to. Smart businesspeople order mineral water, not wine, at their business lunches.

Being fat, in fact, can cause real problems for an American. He or she will find it harder to get a good job, or even to make friends. If you want to do well, you must be thin. It doesn't seem fair, does it? Advertisers and fast-food sellers scream at people to eat, eat, eat. But inside, there is another voice saying "stop, stop, stop."

A food seller in New York City

Popcorn—a favorite American snack

Heat 1 tablespoon of vegetable oil in a deep, heavy pan.
Add 1 oz/25 grams of dried corn kernels (maize). Cover with a lid and shake the pan.
The corn will start to "pop." Take the pan off the heat when all the corn has popped.
Sprinkle with salt or sugar and serve.

Ellen Logan at the Holiday Inn

I'm sure you've heard of the "Big Apple." It's what they call New York City, at the heart of which lies Manhattan Island. But I'm also sure you've never heard of the "Little Apple." It's a much smaller Manhattan, in the state of Kansas, almost exactly in the middle of America.

For a small town, Manhattan, Kansas has some big surprises. And one of them is the Holiday Inn hotel, with rooms built around a swimming pool and a friendly family atmosphere.

The Holiday Inn is where Manhattan people often go for a special party, or a night out. A lot of them choose to eat in the brightly lit restaurant near the pool. And many of them will be served by Ellen Logan, who has worked as a waitress here for more than two years.

Ellen, like most of the waitresses, is also a student. She comes from Nebraska, but she's studying at Kansas State University, just outside Manhattan. She's planning one day to be a veterinary surgeon, and to care for small animals. But in order to support herself at college, she works twenty hours a week at the Holiday Inn.

Ellen soon learned what every waitress finds out. Your best friend is a good pair of shoes. She paid forty-five dollars for hers, much more than she would usually spend. She's discovered something else too. You don't have to know much about food to be a good waitress, but you do have to know a lot about people.

"A lot of businesspeople always stay here when they come to Manhattan," she explains. "They like you to recognize them and remember their favorite dishes. But some couples come for a night out together. They just want to be left alone. Then there are people who can't make up their minds. They look down the menu and say 'What do you suggest?' So I ask them how hungry they are. If they say, 'Not very,' I suggest the salad bar, with soup, salad, bread, and a fruit plate. But if they say they're very hungry, I suggest a Kansas Strip Steak, with potatoes or rice. You get salad and bread as well. It's very nice. Real good value."

Ellen may get tired feet sometimes, but at least she's never bored. She's learning too much about people. She'll probably make a good animal doctor, but if she finds she doesn't like it after all, she can always become a psychiatrist instead.

Bend, Stretch, and Spend

"Americans are not as fit as they think they are," says Dr. Michael McGinnis of the U.S. Department of Health and Human Services. That should come as a surprise, because in the U.S., fitness is something you cannot get away from. You'll see special stores selling clothes for exercise. You'll find the stores full of books and cassettes telling you how to get fit. You'll meet joggers in the park, and find at least one health club in every town.

But the figures don't look too good. More than 30 percent of Americans smoke, and 80 to 90 percent still don't get enough exercise. The situation is worse among children, who spend too much time watching TV, and too little time running around.

The American diet, too, is less than perfect. Quick, ready-made food usually contains too much fat, salt, and sugar. And, as usual, it's the poorest families who eat the worst food. Eating well means spending what they don't have—more time and more money.

Right:
Out for an early morning run

Americans know they have a fitness problem. Many people feel they are too fat, even if their doctors disagree. And 80 percent of people say they try to improve their fitness, even if they soon give up.

Good exercise, like a good diet, can be expensive. That's why the fast-growing fitness industry caters mostly to middle-class people. The super-rich, of course, can spend what they like to get fit in style. Stars like Sylvester Stallone, Superman Christopher Reeve, and Linda Evans from the TV series "Dynasty" have their own trainers. There are no gym clubs or public swimming pools for them. They get the personal care of an expert, wherever and whenever they feel like bending and stretching.

You don't have to have a personal trainer to spend money on fitness. In the mid-1980s, Americans were spending a billion dollars a year on exercise equipment. Perhaps you think that at least running is free? Certainly not. Americans spend over 150 million dollars a year on running suits.

There's a growing interest in cycling in the States. Surely that, at least, is cheap, once you have paid for your bike? Not at all. Fashion

comes on two wheels too. Cycling clothes are selling as they never have before. One specialist is the Bicycle Outfitter in Los Altos, California. They sell suits, gloves, shoes, jerseys, sunglasses, and everything the cyclist could want. The only thing they don't sell is—bicycles.

Polaki— Fitness Trainer

"Press your right hand all the way up to the ceiling, and push, now your left hand, push up! And here we go, it's a one and a two and a three and four! Now bend right over and press your hands down to the floor. Straighten your knees, now start pulling up. OK! Relax!"

The pretty woman in the pink exercise suit is very glad to stop. For over an hour, Polaki has been making her exercise every muscle in her body, and now she's tired. One hour a day is quite enough for her. But for Polaki, three or four hours of exercising is quite normal. It's part of her job as a fitness trainer.

Polaki starts her day early. By six o'clock she has ridden across San Francisco on her powerful motorbike and is ready for her first appointment, with a busy and successful businesswoman.

"People don't enjoy seeing me so early in the morning," says Polaki. "But they're usually smiling when I go."

Polaki always does the exercises with her clients. "Sometimes, if I'm really tired, I stop," she says, "but as soon as they see that I've stopped, they stop too." Usually, though, Polaki is happy to carry on. She feels much better when she's in shape.

"Exercise is good for everything, for your mind and your body," she says. "I feel bad-tempered if I don't exercise for a few days."

Some of her millionaire clients feel the same way. Sometimes they discover they cannot manage without her when they fly off around the world. Polaki may find she has to rush suddenly to Venice or Vienna, just to spend a few hours making one of her clients do her exercises.

Exercise has always been important to Polaki. She started her career as a jazz dancer, but she broke her back in a climbing accident. After that she kept fit by doing exercises instead. A wealthy friend with a weight problem asked Polaki to teach her the exercises too. The woman lost eighty pounds, and soon her friends were calling Polaki's number. The business grew from there.

Her way of life suits Polaki. She likes to be free and independent. She doesn't bother to think about the future.

"I just live for today," she says. "I don't want marriage and kids. I go along with the flow of the stream. Life is like reading a story. It's fun to turn a page and see what's going to happen next."

Polaki (in white) with one of her clients

Exercises

1 **Match the following and list them in the correct boxes below.**

Bears
Browns
Chicago
Cincinnati
Detroit
Jets
Kansas City
New York
Pittsburgh
Reds
Royals
Steelers
St. Louis
Tigers
Add any other teams you know,
including any from other sports,
e.g. basketball.

	City	Name of Team
Baseball		
Football		
Other		

2 **Match the description with the festival.**

1 Thanksgiving Day
2 Passover
3 Halloween
4 Mardi Gras
5 St. Patrick's Day
6 Burns Night
7 Chinese New Year

a) People follow a dancing lion through the streets.
b) People with Scottish ancestors drink whisky and listen to bagpipe music.
c) American families meet for a special dinner and remember the Pilgrim Fathers.
d) Celebrated by Jewish people.
e) Celebrated by people in New Orleans.
f) A day when Chicago turns green.
g) Children try to frighten their neighbors into giving them good things to eat.

3 **Fill each space with one of the words given below.**

or have a baby   as well as the great holidays   as well as soap operas   except when they are at school

1 Few Americans actually take part in ballgames, ...

2 Most Americans celebrate festivals which have a meaning for a special religious or national group,

. . . . which all Americans share.

3 In America, your friends organize a "shower" for you if you marry . . . .

4 Hollywood studios produce films which people go to movie theaters to see,

. . . . which they watch at home.

4 **Discussion**

1 Are American eating habits very different from those in your own country? Are people in your own country also eating more and more "fast food"?

2 Do you think work on "smile repair" and tightening loose skin is a good use of dentists' and doctors' skills and time?

3 Do Americans make good use of their leisure time? Do they work too hard, or have too much leisure time?